ΛPPΛLΛCHIΛN
REVIEW

VOL. 49, NO. 2
SPRING 2021

TRADITION. DIVERSITY. CHANGE.

©2021 by Berea College. Vol. 49, No. 2, Spring 2021. All rights reserved. No part of this publication may be reproduced without the prior permission of *Appalachian Review*. Periodicals postage paid at Berea, Kentucky, and at additional mailing offices. ISSN# 03632318.

CONTENTS

INTERVIEW

BOOK REVIEWS

COVER PHOTOGRAPH
Garden Guardian by Carey Gough

EDITOR'S NOTE

JASON KYLE HOWARD

Kinship. It's a theme that is always vital and relevant, no matter the times and trends. As readers, we are always interested in relationships: with family, with friends, with romantic partners, with office colleagues, with institutions, with nature. With the world writ large. And now, in our time of pandemic, as we amble towards a sense of recovery and normality with the widespread prevalence of—and unfortunately, skepticism and hostility towards—vaccinations, kinship once again stands at the forefront of our minds.

After fourteen months in lockdown—after having plenty of time to reevaluate our priorities and needs, after observing cavalier and reckless behavior—many of us are rethinking and even renegotiating our relationships, just like many of the characters from the prose found in this issue. In an exclusive excerpt from Shawna Kay Rodenberg's debut memoir *Kin*, she recalls a scene from her childhood with her family, and particularly her father, while living in an End Times, off-the-grid commune that lays the groundwork for such a reassessment. Erin Miller Reid's story "Adrift" depicts a college-aged narrator who, while studying abroad in 1980s West Germany—thousands of miles from her Kentucky home—is sizing up her relationships. Likewise, Laura Marshall's story "The Lost and Found Museum" offers an original, compelling portrait of a place and relationships seemingly frozen in time. In an aching lyric essay, acclaimed novelist Elaine Neil Orr reflects on her relationship with her body and the aging process, while award-winning essayist Jake Maynard assesses his personal—and our cultural—relationship with the banjo, race, and history in his essay "This American Fife."

In a startling, visceral set of poems, Laura Neal offers readers what she terms a "perspective...across time, space, race and age with an attempt to exploit the 'everyday'", of noting what "often [goes] unnoted." Natasha Pepperl turns her keen eye towards what she calls "Ceremonies of Family", and poets Carolyn Wilsey and Adam Tavel offer ekphrastic responses to works of art.

Of writing her memoir *Kin*, Rodenberg observes in our conversation that "the mindful preservation of my own history has given me a sense at times of having been made whole again, or of things being 'set to rights,' as my mom used to say." That, too, might describe where many of us find ourselves with our kith and kin—questioning, asserting, embracing, loving, leaving, renewing—now, certainly, but always. ◼

2020 DENNY C. PLATTNER AWARDS

The annual Plattner Awards were established in 1995 by Kenneth and Elissa Plattner to honor their late son and his love of writing. The awards are given to the finest pieces of fiction, creative nonfiction, and poetry that appeared in *Appalachian Review* during the previous year. Winners receive a $200 prize, and both winners and honorable mentions are awarded a handsome piece of handmade ceramics designed and manufactured by Berea College Crafts.

FICTION
Judged by Karen Salyer McElmurray, author of
Wanting Radiance *and* The Motel of the Stars

Winner: Vanessa Van Besien, "Milk"
Honorable Mention: Jayne Moore Waldrop, "For What It's Worth"

CREATIVE NONFICTION
Judged by Shawna Kay Rodenberg, author of Kin: A Memoir

Winner: Kathleen Driskell, "Keats In Your Time of Pandemic"
Honorable Mention: Denise Giardina, "Socks & Junior"

POETRY
Judged by Jeremy Paden, author of
World as Sacred Burning Heart *and* Broken Tulips

Winner: "Gone" by L. Renée
Honorable Mention: "The River" by Benjamin Cutler

RAKE

While the lowlands were still hazel
beneath an early sun,
I'd lift my head to the harsh
crackle of leaves,
steadied by my mother's hands,
only one of them gloved.
And I watched, before rising, a woman gather
by wielding her body, combing
through the soil rake-like,
thinking now, how a rake
can be made of a woman,
a hay-bound hell raiser
bending to collect the frizzled grasses,
shift them into weightless piles
until the fields were smoothed over
the rake leaning against the pine, leaves in its teeth.

LAURA NEAL

TRYING TO GET OUT OF THE WOODS

the floor is messy
relentless
as a crouching fire

around here somewhere
is a snake

I can smell
something suffering
tantrum hum of insect

I'm not a hunter

around here somewhere
something alive
is swallowed

summer has cracked
the ground
nothing plucking up
butterflies are ghost

this—is a land of task

around here somewhere
there's a sharp hole
gathering angled branches
and ankle bones

LAURA NEAL

IN SICKNESS

The devil is beating his wife today,
my grandmother says it happens when
rain falls while the sun is out.

Our clothes are out on the line.
My mother meant to grab them
but she grabbed hold of me
placing a cool rag atop my forehead
my vomit on the side of the sheets.

Heavy as the hog in Uncle Albert's pen
my snout dripping and hot.
I'm more trouble than I'm worth.

We try to heal it on our own,
the spicy mustard slathered
in the middle of my chest,
to pull whatever was in me out.

&

I hear the rain slamming down the window
the wind whipping against the weedy bush.

She has cakes in the oven, a bowl of batter
waiting to fill the pan. There are dresses to sew,
pants to be hemmed. The floors need to be swept,
vacuumed, mopped, the trash, taken out and burned.
Then there's my sister's hair, the box of chicken to clean
and a husband to feed.

&

I feel my burden.
The weight of those clothes upon my shoulders,
the splinter in my mother's back.

I imagine myself hanging up there from that tree,
being let out to dry, the sweat of my brow
slipping its way to the corner of my mouth.
I know she doesn't blame me for all the other times,
not even this time, but I should have been there,
if only to grab the clothes from the line.

When the storm scatters, she slides back the curtain
letting sunlight drown the room. Up in the pine,
her white blouse. She swears, lets out a sigh
that would bruise a plum, the storm
brought to rest in her face.

LAURA NEAL

THREE BIRDS

There is only one window in the kitchen
where a chicken is being fried in peanut oil
its meat peppered and salted.

I lift the glass on the front door
trying to air out the house
from the choking smoke.

I sit on the wooden step. Here,
I still hear the popping applause of the grease
a beckoning of sorts
a call to feast.

Beyond the yard, I see a deer,
dead behind a line of pines.

Buzzards circle, first two, then four,
then nine, wheeling near the deer.

I watch the way they tear at what's dead.

Ripping at a flesh-piece
large enough to lift away somewhere,
the blood flouring the air.

We too favor our meat fresh.
Deer from the local road.
Chicken straight from the coop.

I can *just* smell the carcass,
the meat left soiling
in the pitch of last night.

At night, I graze outside
everyone wandering off
to their own rooms.

And I dream. Not about flying like a bird,
but falling like one.

LAURA NEAL

BOUND

I can't walk away from here
the place I call home.
It's tethered within me.
Everywhere I go I take
with me a story
of some dusty old field
in a lonely small town
where over in the plains
just at the point the grasses
meet the trees
I watch a deer
not expecting me to be still
not expecting me to be weaponless.
I'm too compelled
to tell how I saw a union of wasps
jamming themselves
antennae first into glass,
and that in some ways
I can relate, always banging
my head against a door
the sound barely audible.
I want to walk away from there
to hear a different story
one with a different history
one with a different storm.
Tired of all these pointed steps
fatigued in this dizzy sun.

LAURA NEAL

ADRIFT

ERIN MILLER REID

When Georgeanna first arrived in Mainz, the German students assessed her shoes. She wore a pair of Reebok sneakers she'd taken great pains to keep snow white, at times even scrubbing the soles with Comet cleaning powder. "You can always know an American by their shoes," a classmate said in accented English. "They wear sneakers everywhere, not just to do sport." His English was far better than

Georgeanna's German, even though she was the one spending two semesters abroad. The next day she wore her brown loafers instead, complete with a shiny copper penny wedged in the slit just over the tongue. "Those shoes look like something my Oma would wear," a female classmate said with brusque German-bred honesty that Georgeanna would eventually learn to not take personally.

After class, Georgeanna took a bus downtown, its wide body weaving with hisses and sighs between timber-lined buildings that hovered along narrow streets originally intended for pushcarts and wagons, never vehicles the size of single-wide mobile homes. Georgeanna stared at the bus's floor appraising the shoes of other passengers. Indeed, the elderly ladies, their wheeled produce baskets in tow, wore loafers. Georgeanna reasoned that her own penny loafers were sleeker and daintier than the heavy-soled sort West German senior citizens wore. However, she noticed that the girls closer to her age sported heels of all types—strappy and close-toed, rounded and squared, mostly sleek black and dark brown— but all with height. At the department store, Georgeanna chose a chocolate-brown pair of lace-up, platform Oxfords. She caught her heels on cracked sidewalks at first, and her ankles ached at the end of the day, but no one commented on how American she looked anymore, or how she resembled a grandmother.

That was months ago. Now Georgeanna managed the sidewalks of West Germany in heels with confidence. She expertly navigated the cobblestone streets of downtown without stumbling. She raced up the stairwell when she was late for class, and climbed the library stepladder to reach books on the top shelf.

Her honed skills of heel-wearing were put to the test in one of the wooded thickets tucked in and around the campus. Georgeanna admired the German penchant for nature, and these woods, as small as they were, reminded her of the tree-covered hills back home in Kentucky, where the forests were dense with pines, poplars, and an underbrush of rhododendron, creeper vine, and fallen trunks that she and her siblings, Elena and P.J. spent entire days exploring as kids.

Georgeanna sat down on a cement bench in the otherwise empty grove to eat an apple and write a letter to her boyfriend Trent. She took a bite of the apple, so juicy that it dripped onto her chin, and scribbled away to Trent, assuring him that despite the good time she was having and all she was learning, she still loved him and missed him. She sunk her front teeth into another mouthful of apple. The crack of the apple's crisp flesh pierced the quiet that had settled in the crop of birch trees and alders. A pigeon scuttled from under the bench and pecked at her feet. Just as Georgeanna bit a tiny morsel of apple to toss to the bird, a completely naked man emerged from the bushes. He blinked as if his eyes were adjusting to the first sun of the day. He was bald from head to toe, no hair on his head, his chest, his arms, or legs. His penis hung unadorned by even the smallest tuft. His skin was pale, like the buttermilk Georgeanna used to dunk leftover cornbread into for an afterschool snack. *The Naktbader.* She'd only heard about the campus nudist from other students. She'd never seen him herself. According to student lore, he was a graduate school drop-out who camped out in the nooks and crannies of the campus, ate from the cafeteria dumpster, and bathed in the central fountain at odd hours of the night. Students debated his hairless physique, whether it was self-induced with a razor or due to a rare disease.

Georgeanna's eyes locked with the startled stare of the *Naktbader.* He stood stone still, like a cornered rabbit gauging its escape. Georgeanna gasped. She wanted to scream, but no sound came. Instead, she dropped her apple and Trent's letter and sprinted from the woods. She skipped over unearthed tree roots and dodged jutted stones. As she ran, she felt the man's eyes follow her. She took the steps to her dorm room by twos, and locked her bedroom door behind her. She leaned her full weight against the door, anxious that the man had chased her, that at any moment he would pound on her door and jiggle the knob. Outside, the branch of a linden tree scraped her window. She crossed the room and looked outside. Only two students walked to class. There was no naked man charging her dorm. After the pounding of her heart eased, and after she caught her breath, she smiled, impressed by how agilely she'd run in her stacked heels. Who needed sneakers? Once she'd calmed down completely, she sat down at the desk and rewrote her letter to Trent.

After the pounding of her heart eased, and after she caught her breath, she smiled, impressed by how agilely she'd run in her stacked heels. Who needed sneakers?

His reply came two weeks later. Georgeanna read it as she clopped along the bicycle path to visit Herr Schneider at the old folks home. She was careful to hug the shrub-line to avoid an angry ring from a bicycle bell, or a cyclist hollering, *Pass auf!*

Trent's letter was exactly what she should have expected, especially since she'd made the mistake of telling him about her encounter with the *Naktbader*. The patronizing, anxious tone reminded her of the letters he'd written before she ever left the States. As soon as she announced that she'd applied for the German study abroad program last spring, Trent's missives arrived in her campus P.O. box once a week like clockwork, warning her about every possible risk of studying abroad. Gypsy pick-pockets, terrorists, hepatitis, airplane crashes, malaria, human smugglers, food poisoning. Each time, Georgeanna wrote back, *West Germany isn't a third-world country. It's as safe as America. Don't worry, I'll come home to you safe and sound.*

Georgeanna tucked the letter in her jacket pocket. If anything, she was endeared by Trent's devotion. He'd loved her intensely since they were both fifteen. Trent's letter also amused her. He knew so little about the world beyond the borders of southeast Kentucky, beyond gravel roads and reclaimed strip mines, beyond the front row pew and potluck casseroles made with too much cream of mushroom soup. Why, Trent still considered the stilted English of the King James Bible, the *thees* and *thous* and *haths*, a foreign language. He had never truly left home, instead studying at a small Baptist college twenty minutes up Highway 25, while Georgeanna had gone to a state school hours away.

Georgeanna reached the old folks' home and pushed through the double glass doors. The lobby was still. A lone elderly woman in a housecoat shuffled across the linoleum floor with her walker. The lobby smelled like the overripe bananas kept in a fruit bowl next to a pitcher of water on the counter. The bananas never looked touched, changing from greenish yellow at the first of the week to brown-speckled ripeness by Saturday, always six in the bunch.

Georgeanna signed her name in a guest book. The front desk clerk nodded at her. By now, she was familiar to all the desk staff since she visited Herr Schneider at least once a week. Georgeanna liked to believe that she visited him because she genuinely wanted to do something to help out a lonely, elderly man, but deep down she knew she was using the visits to check a box on her medical school application. She wanted to be a doctor like her dad, and medical schools liked students who had ample hours of volunteer service.

Honestly, Georgeanna wasn't sure her visits made much of a difference to Herr Schneider. Most of the time he sat in his green tweed armchair watching television, while Georgeanna sat on a wooden chair she moved from the tiny two-seater kitchen table. She'd occasionally ask questions, but mostly Herr Schneider would ramble on in half-hearted monologues while a soccer game or the evening news blared in the background, the television's volume always too loud. He never looked at Georgeanna, but fixed his milky blue eyes, magnified by black-framed Coke bottle lenses, on the sliding glass door that led to a sun porch littered with mismatched flower pots full of overgrown, rangy herbs. A tarnished wind chime hung above the dill, thyme, marjoram, and parsley, ringing tinny and anemic with even the slightest breeze.

At first, Georgeanna had barely understood Herr Schneider. He spoke in a Hessian dialect. His words weren't sharp and pointed like other German speakers, but instead lumped on his tongue like a mouthful of mashed potatoes. Georgeanna spoke with an accent herself—*country, hillbilly* —something that had been pointed out to her many times at her college in Louisville. The city was farther north than Wickers Bend, and accents like hers weren't as common in that part of the state. "Say kite. Say bite. Say ice cream," her classmates had prodded her. She'd oblige, and all those words came out as *cat, bat,* and *ass cream.* That last one especially received lots of laughs. Georgeanna tried to ignore their motives, and just assumed they were laughing at the novelty of her accent and not at her.

With practice, Georgeanna understood Herr Schneider's Hessian German. She learned that he was ninety-two. His wife had died two decades ago, and he still missed her. He had no children of his own, only a stepson who visited once a year on

Christmas Eve. Herr Schneider considered the man useless. "Doesn't even have a job. He always asks me for money. Me! A poor man. Such a *Nichtnutz*, that boy," he'd lament every time the subject of his stepson came up. Herr Schneider had grown up on a steamboat with his parents and six siblings sailing up and down the Rhine River delivering coal. He claimed he never once stepped foot inside a school room, though he learned to read from an older sister. Georgeanna had noticed the only book in Herr Schneider's apartment was a dust-covered Bible on the television stand.

She knocked on Herr Schneider's door. Some of the residents adorned their apartment doors with flowered wreaths or wooden placards that read *Wilkommen*. Herr Schneider's door was plain, except for a single scratch down the center that marred the oak stain. As usual, Herr Scheneider immediately invited her in. "*Kommen Sie rein,*" he called, as if he'd been waiting for her to knock. It reminded Georgeanna of her Sunday calls home.

Each week, she bought a calling card that cost five Marks from the gas station. The card advertised that she could call the United States for two Pfennigs per minute, which should have amounted to 250 minutes, but after exchange rates and connection fees, she never got more than twenty. Her dad always picked up after the first ring, just like Herr Schneider called out so quickly after a single knock. Georgeanna imagined her dad sitting at the kitchen table, the phone on the wall just above him, waiting for her call every Sunday afternoon at two p.m. Kentucky time, eight p.m. in West Germany. Then her mom, dad, and P.J., her little brother, the only kid still at home, would pass the phone back and forth. She'd tell her dad about her classwork and assure her mother she was eating well and saying her nightly prayers, and then she'd talk the longest to P.J., telling him all about her new friends and weekend travels and hearing about his basketball season and who he was taking to Homecoming. She and P.J. were especially close despite a six-year age difference.

Georgeanna stepped into Herr Schneider's low-lit apartment. The curtains were pulled across the sliding glass doors to keep the glare off the television. Herr Schneider watched a soccer game at full volume. "*Guten Tag*," Georgeanna greeted the old man who barely leaned forward in his armchair to acknowledge her. "*Tag*," he answered, abruptly. A dirty pan with crumbs of charred sausage sat on the stove. Georgeanna washed it and the other dishes in the sink before she sat down.

Herr Schneider gestured at the thirteen-inch television screen fuming over a penalty. "*Schade*," Georgeanna said. It was the generic German word for *That's a pity*. She didn't know what else to say. Whenever Herr Schneider complained, which he did often—about soccer games, politics, the nursing aids at the home, his wayward stepson, his joints— Georgeanna simply said *Schade*.

Today, Georgeanna wished Herr Schneider would say anything, even if it was complaining. Instead, for the next ten minutes he focused on the television and was mute except for an occasional grunt. The silence between them felt awkward.

Georgeanna fidgeted with the zipper of her jacket. She wished the apartment wasn't so dark so that she could sweep Herr Schneider's floor, or that there were more dishes in the sink to wash, anything to do to make herself useful. Then she remembered her weekend excursion to Sankt Goarshausen. She and two dormmates had hiked to the Lorelei rock last Sunday. Of course, Georgeanna had worn her Reeboks for the excursion instead of her heels. The climb was steep, winding up the side of the mountain in a series of rough-hewn rock steps. Even young and fit, she and her friends had to take breaks. At the top of the mountain, they were rewarded with a bird's eye view of the Rhine, snaking between cliffs and sheer mountainsides. An alabaster statue of Lorelei sat at the top. Moss grew in the crooks of her elbows and in the folds of her gown. Her carved eyes with no pupils or irises stared the river below, unflinching for decades.

"Did you ever see Lorelei?" Georgeanna asked Herr Schneider on a whim. "Did you ever hear her voice when you sailed the Rhine?"

"*Ach ja, die Lorelei*," Herr Schneider lifted his eyes from the television screen and gave a rare smile. "I never saw or heard her, but I knew a man that did." He told her about the boat of a bachelor, a sailor his family knew from their work on the river. The bachelor's ship crashed into the rocks at the base of Lorelei's cliff, splintering its wooden hull and dumping barrels of flour, boxes of linen, and coal into the water. The bachelor's body was never found, but his deck cat survived by climbing

An alabaster statue of Lorelei sat at the top. Moss grew in the crooks of her elbows and in the folds of her gown. Her carved eyes with no pupils or irises stared at the river below, unflinching for decades.

onto the jagged scree. Herr Schneider's father rescued the cat and named him *Glück*, Luck.

Herr Schneider retold the legend of Lorelei to Georgeanna. She humored him by listening and nodding intently, though she already knew all about the siren, a jilted lover, who sat at the top of a cliff and sang with a lilting voice so that sailors would wreck at the mountain's craggy base. Lorelei was a bitter beauty with a vendetta against men.

"My wife took me off the river before Lorelei could get me," Herr Schneider said. "She didn't want me gone all the time on the boat. So, I got a job as a painter. Painted houses, painted shops, painted school buildings."

"Did you like it?" Georgeanna asked.

"*Nein*," Herr Schneider answered. "It was boring. I only got fresh air when I worked outside jobs. The paint fumes made me feel thick-headed."

"*Schade*," Georgeanna said, pondering what it would mean to pick the wrong profession and work your entire life doing something you despised.

"I always liked the jobs that used blue paint though," Herr Schneider said, "any shade of blue. The color reminded me of the river." He took off his glasses and perched them lens-side up on his knee, then rubbed both eyes with his knobby, rheumatic knuckles. He sighed, a weary, world-worn sigh, and laid his head against the back of the armchair.

"Herr Schneider, are you okay?" Georgeanna leaned forward in the wooden chair.

"*Ja, ja*. I'm just tired. I want a nap." Not one for social formalities, the old man didn't even open his eyes as he spoke.

It was a chance for Georgeanna to excuse herself, even if she'd only stayed fifteen minutes. Her visit today had to be short anyway. She was meeting a friend tonight, and wanted enough time to freshen her hair and make-up. She was giddy about the evening, and anxious about how it might unfold. As she left Herr Schneider's apartment, Georgeanna noticed that all the walls of the old folks' home were painted vanilla, the color generally chosen to avoid plain white. She wished the walls were blue for Herr Schneider's sake.

■ ■ ■

At seven p.m., Georgeanna met Alex at the bus stop on the curb at the edge of campus. Alex, the same classmate who'd first called attention to the foreignness of her sneakers all those months ago, had asked her to see a band with him. Georgeanna had never been out alone with a guy other than Trent, and on that evening, she reassured herself over and over that she and Alex were just two friends going to a concert, that this wasn't an actual date. They rode on the bus side-by-side, their shoulders pressing together with each sharp turn and their thighs grazing every time the bus eased to the edge of the street to let passengers on and off.

The concert venue was a concrete amphitheater in a park on the bank of the Rhine. They met up with a few of Alex's friends, college-aged boys wearing AC/DC and Def Leppard T-shirts. The guys immediately clapped each other on the back. *"Wie geht's? Was ist los?"*

Georgeanna hung back until Alex introduced her. *"Hallo,* pleased to meet you" his friends greeted her with awkward, business-like handshakes, then immediately started chatting in rapid-fire German. Georgeanna didn't understand all the words and slang phrases, but was able to deduce that Alex was going to buy beers for the group. With Alex's friends deep in conversation about music and bands, Georgeanna sat on the ground and waited. She fingered the blades of grass that poked at her ankles. If she didn't look across the barge-clogged river toward the opposite shore's cockeyed tower, a crumbling remnant from Roman conquests; if she blocked out the background chatter garnished with unfamiliar, throaty inflections; if she didn't smell the sizzling juices from the rotisserie lamb that Turkish immigrants sliced for kebabs at the food wagon; if she only focused on those blades of grass— she might think she was still in Wickers Bend sitting by the creek in her back yard.

Alex returned to the group, balancing four plastic cups of beer, the white froth spilling over the edges and dripping from his fingers. His friends took the first two beers. Alex sat down next to Georgeanna and handed her the remaining cup, then wiped his wet hand on the grass.

"*Prost*," Alex tapped the rim of his cup to hers, and they both drank. Georgeanna licked the froth from her upper lip. The beer didn't taste as bitter as she'd expected. She was thirsty and took another gulp, guzzling down half the cup. Alex laughed when she pulled her lips from the rim and exhaled. "You're a fish," he said. Georgeanna blushed, relishing the sweet, yeasty aftertaste.

Even though she and Alex had been in class together for months, they hadn't spoken much. He sat in the back row, close to the door so he could dart out between classes for smoke breaks. She sat in the front of the room so she could

He prodded her to speak English, but she resisted. "I can only learn German if I practice."

closely watch the professor's lips as he spoke, hoping she wouldn't miss a word. Alex asked Georgeanna about herself. She answered with short sentences and simplistic phrases, her nerves showing in her floundering language skills. She asked Alex questions that she'd mastered in German class, even though they made her feel like a third-grader getting to know her bunkmate at summer camp. *How old are you? Do you have brothers and sisters? What's your favorite sport?* When Georgeanna didn't understand Alex or couldn't adequately answer his question, she smiled. He prodded her to speak English, but she resisted. "I can only learn German if I practice."

Midway through the band's first set, Alex went to get more beer. While she waited, Georgeanna thought about her call home to her brother P.J. tomorrow night. She couldn't wait to tell him she'd gone out with Alex, that she'd drunk more than a few sips of beer. He'd be proud of her. She remembered one of their late-night conversations last summer before she left. While she relaxed on the bed thumbing through an old copy of *Seventeen*, P.J. sat at her desk his feet propped against her mattress and tilting the wooden chair on its two back legs. Their sister Elena, also home from college but not a night owl like her siblings, lay asleep on the floor, curled up under an orange and brown afghan.

That night, P.J. had grilled Georgeanna about college life—how hard the classes were, if she ever saw the basketball players around campus, if the girls were much prettier than the ones in Wickers Bend. He also asked her about the nightlife, and chided her when she said she'd only been to a few frat parties and found all the drunk guys passed out in the bushes disappointing. "*Disappointing*," P.J. mocked her. "You're such a prude, Georgeanna. Lighten up and have some fun. You only live once."

Her boyfriend Trent was the main reason she didn't go out much at home. He was straight-laced, and since she was his girlfriend, Georgeanna tried to follow suit. In high school, she once tried Jim Beam at a party. As soon as it crossed her lips, her mouth burned. The liquor's heat expanded, filling the spaces between her teeth and creeping along her palate to the back of her throat. She grimaced and spat it out onto the grass. Her tongue tingled even without the whiskey in her mouth. Trent saw her take the sip straight from the bottle. He marched over and wrested her by the elbow from her group of friends. "Georgeanna, we're better than that. We don't need to get drunk at parties to feel cool." He'd leaned into her face, speaking through a clenched jaw, the same way her mom had reprimanded her for coloring on the carpet as a four-year-old.

She'd seen the look in his eyes before, like he could throw her to the ground if he wanted but never would because he was too principled. He'd been anchored to a church pew every Sunday since he wore diapers. He was taught that a man should never raise a hand to a woman. The duty of a man was to protect a woman, and that's what he was doing, protecting her from wrongdoing.

Georgeanna knew how to diffuse him. That night at the house party she wriggled her elbow from his fist, and scooped her shoulder just under his armpit, pressing her chest against his ribs. "I just wanted a taste, Trent. I was curious." Georgeanna hugged him. "You're right though. I shouldn't have done that. I love you." She pecked her boyfriend on the neck, and the tight muscles loosened at once under the pressure of her lips.

P.J. hated Trent, and he would be thrilled, vindicated even, that Georgeanna had spent time with another guy. If she told P.J. about this date tomorrow, two p.m. Kentucky time, eight p.m. West German time, she'd make him swear to not breathe a word of it to another soul.

When Alex returned with the beer, he handed Georgeanna a cup and sat back down on the grass, this time so close that when he rested his elbows on bent knees, Georgeanna could smell the piney scent of his deodorant. When she again gulped down the foamy head of the beer, the edge of her layered bangs slipped into the froth. Alex pulled the hair from her cup, wiped her hair clean, and then tucked it behind her ear.

Georgeanna smiled at him, a warm glow filling her belly, her head light like a helium balloon. It must be the beer. She'd never drunk this much before. Alex smiled back, then rested his hand on top of hers, his fingers folding into her palm. Georgeanna froze, then jerked her hand to her lap. "I have a boyfriend," she blurted out.

Alex gave a single embarrassed laugh and leaned back on his arms. "Of course you do," he said in English. He angled his body away from her. Georgeanna felt a twinge of regret, though she wasn't even sure if Alex was her type. She already knew, just sitting at this concert with the screeching electric guitars, the throb of drums, and the staccato disco lights transforming the stage into a pulsating rainbow, that they didn't share the same taste in music.

She wondered whether Trent was her type either. He was the only boyfriend she'd ever had. Trent was an Eagle Scout, their high school's record holder for the 800-meter, and an all-A engineering student. He was the guy any girl would choose, and they'd grown up together. They'd gone to the same Baptist church, studied the same Biology and English courses in high school, competing with each other for the top grades in the class. They ran track together, though Georgeanna had done it more for exercise than competition. It had always seemed she and Trent just belonged together. She'd never questioned it until she was thousands of miles away across an ocean being shunned by a guy she wasn't sure she liked as any more than just a friend.

Georgeanna remembered another night in her bedroom last summer. It was the night before she left for her trip. Trent came to the Sutton's house to hang out while Georgeanna finished packing. As she sifted through a pile of T-shirts, jeans, make-up, and snapshots of her friends and family, trying to decide what to take along in those last empty pockets and crevices of her suitcase, Trent leaned back on her bed against a chenille pillow and watched her. "I'm still not sure about you taking this trip," he said as Georgeanna tucked one more pair of jeans into her luggage.

"I've been planning to study abroad for years," Georgeanna said. "This is my dream. You should be happy for me."

"I'll just worry about you," he said, "It doesn't seem quite right traveling all over the world, especially all alone."

"I'll be careful, Trent. I won't go places by myself at night."

"It's not just that," he paused, tracing his fingers over a ceramic, pixie-faced cheerleader dressed in a red and black uniform, their high school colors. It had been a gift to Georgeanna from Trent's mom, even though Georgeanna had never been on the cheer squad. "I just wonder what's there that you don't have here at home. I worry you'll come back and not want me."

Georgeanna stood up and circled the end of the bed, stepping over mounds of stuff on the floor. "Trent, don't worry," she said, cupping his jaw in her palm. She lifted one leg to straddle his lap on the bed, and then kissed his forehead, his cheeks, his neck.

When his hands lifted her shirt, when his fingertips crept under the cup of her bra, when he unzipped her jeans, she didn't stop him. When he flipped her on her back, she didn't ask him to stop. The pain was sharp, and the whole act was lightning fast. When Trent collapsed on her, she bit her lip and started to cry. "I'm sorry, Trent."

His back rose and fell with heavy breaths. He lifted up on his forearms to look at her. "It's okay," he said, his voice still ragged. "We'll be married someday Georgeanna. We won't do it again until we're married."

That was last summer, and Georgeanna had figured out since then that sleeping with your boyfriend once was not necessarily an engagement. Georgeanna side-eyed Alex. He joked with his buddies and ignored her. She admired the way his hair flopped over his forehead, how his skin flushed in a ruddy horseshoe on his cheek, how he'd taken the chance and asked out the foreign girl. She finished her beer and picked at the blades of grass under her palms.

After the concert, Alex and Georgeanna rode back to campus together. Georgeanna's buzz had worn off. Alex didn't buy her any more beers after she'd rebuffed him. Now, he sat across the aisle from her in steely silence on the mostly empty bus. Georgeanna thought again about her phone call home tomorrow night. She wouldn't tell P.J. that the night ended with her being sober, and her date fuming two arm lengths away. Instead, she would tell him about the loud rock concert, how a woman in the front row flashed the lead singer, how she could see ancient ruins from her seat on the grass, how the beer's carbonation tickled the roof of her mouth, how she impressed her date by guzzling it down, how she held Alex's hand, how his palm was sweaty. She'd tell P.J. that she was living.

■ ■ ■

The dorm's hallway phone rang at six a.m. the next morning. It woke Georgeanna, though she tried to ignore it as it rang and rang. *Let someone else answer it,* she thought. Finally, her roommate Birgit groaned and rolled from the bed. "*Ich komme,*" she mumbled.

Seconds later Birgit came back to the room, "Georgeanna, it's your mother." Confused, Georgeanna scrambled from the bed. Why would her mother call so early? It was midnight in Kentucky. Her mother should be in bed. Georgeanna's heart thudded as she approached the phone.

"Hello?" Georgeanna gripped the receiver.

Her mother's voice was soft on the other end, hesitant.

"What? How?" Georgeanna shrieked into the hallway phone of the still-dark dormitory, the only light coming from the first rays of sunshine streaming through a window at the end of the corridor. Georgeanna imagined her mom wrapped in a pink velour robe and hunched over the kitchen table, the beige telephone gripped in her slender, always manicured fingers. Georgeanna hoped her dad sat next to her mom, consoling her by rubbing her back. She wondered if Elena was home and sitting at the table with her parents, though she could hardly think of Elena at that kitchen table without P.J. right by her side.

Birgit leaned against the wall next to a bulletin board plastered with flyers advertising pub parties and tutoring services. She stared at Georgeanna, frowning and biting her lip. Mrs. Sutton's voice came in and out as the overseas connection buzzed and crackled. "Mama, I can't hear you," Georgeanna pressed the phone's receiver to her ear, willing the words to come clearly through the earpiece. "What happened to P.J.?"

I'm so sorry. Accident. He's gone. Georgeanna could barely decipher her mother's words. For months, she'd worked to hone her German skills, fumbling over words or nodding to feign comprehension, and now she couldn't understand English either.

"Just get home," her mom said, her voice consumed with staticky sobs. The woman at the other end of the phone line sounded more like a little girl, tiny and fragile, crying over a skinned knee to be kissed, than Georgeanna's mother. This was not the same capable, stoic woman who'd spent Georgeanna's childhood juggling her husband's busy call schedule with her own PTA and library board duties, who had enforced her kids' daily piano practice, who'd mended dresses and attended all of P.J.'s basketball games, all while still setting the table with home-cooked meals made from vegetables canned from their garden. Georgeanna had only seen her mom cry twice. Once, as Georgeanna was being taken back to surgery to remove a near-ruptured appendix, when a single tear dripped from the tip of her mom's nose onto Georgeanna's forehead. The other time was after her grandmother died. Even then, her mom hadn't cried openly in front of the kids. Instead, Georgeanna had seen her sitting at the edge of the creek behind their house, her mom's shoulders quivering in time with the tears.

Georgeanna moved through the next days in a trance. She skipped her classes and booked a flight home, a one-way ticket, unsure if she would be back or not. She packed everything that she couldn't cram in her suitcase—all the books, souvenirs, and new European clothing—into a couple of cardboard boxes marked with her parents' address. If she didn't come back, she'd wire Birgit the money to ship them home.

Home.

She couldn't even imagine it without her little brother there, without his loud mix of Bennie Goodman and David Bowie, Glenn Miller and Pink Floyd that blared from his stereo all hours of the day, without his smelly feet propped on the sofa's armrest on Saturday nights while they watched *SNL* re-runs together during summer vacation. P.J.'s favorite sketch was Roseanne Roseannadanna. Once, he confessed to Georgeanna that he had a crush on Gilda Radner and swore Georgeanna to secrecy. At the time she wondered why it had to be a secret. She figured it out later when she heard P.J. tease his childhood best friend, Sandra, calling her Roseanne Roseannadanna after her hair frizzed in a rainstorm.

■ ■ ■

It was rainy in Germany after P.J. died, three days of constant showers. The bike path was slick and muddy. Georgeanna wobbled and tripped on her way to the old folks' home, her umbrella bouncing and dousing her with rain each time she slipped. She cursed her fashionable heels, and wished she'd opted for her Reeboks instead. She wanted to visit Herr

Schneider one last time. Whether it mattered to the old man or not, she'd feel guilty if she left without saying goodbye. So, even though she had difficulty walking a straight line, even though she was sleep-deprived and her eyes were swollen from crying all night, even though she couldn't hardly think of another soul but P.J., she forged the nasty weather to visit Herr Schneider before she flew home.

Georgeanna shoved her fists into the pockets of her denim jacket. The letter Trent sent last week was still folded inside. Maybe he'd been right. She should have never left home. She should have never come to West Germany. Of course, Trent would be waiting for her back in Wickers Bend. Her dorm

Georgeanna shoved her fists into the pockets of her denim jacket. The letter Trent sent last week was still folded inside. Maybe he'd been right. She should have never left home.

mates had told her he'd called twice since she heard the news about P.J., but she hadn't returned his calls. He'd probably be the one to pick her up from the airport. What would they talk about on the drive home? Would he let her ride in silence?

The lobby of the old folks' home was empty. Georgeanna's was the only umbrella propped against the wall, left to drip a lonely puddle on the floor. There wasn't even an attendant at the desk. Fruit flies swarmed the ripe bananas in the fruit bowl on the counter. Georgeanna's wet shoes squeaked across the linoleum.

She knocked on the door of Herr Schneider's apartment. Inside, a commercial blasted on his television. She listened for his usual prompt response, but nothing. She knocked again, this time louder. Still there was no movement or noise on the other side of the door. Georgeanna jiggled the knob. It was unlocked.

She walked into the apartment with apprehension. It was dark, the only illumination coming from the flash of the television screen. The room smelled of cooked meat and Herr Schneider's pouch of pipe tobacco on the TV tray next to his recliner.

"Herr Schneider? *Wo bist du?* Where are you?" Georgeanna called. She poked her head through the patio doors where the herbs soaked up the morning rain. The wind chimes jangled.

Georgeanna walked back inside and crossed the room to turn off the television. Without the roar of the soccer fans, she heard Herr Schneider's voice, faint and gurgling. He called from the bathroom. "*Hilfe! Hilfe mich!*" Help. Help me.

Georgeanna rushed through the apartment and burst through the bathroom door. Herr Schneider's left arm hung over the edge of the tub, the rest of his body concealed by a white shower curtain. Water dripped from the tips of his fingers, pooling on the tile floor.

"*Hilfe,*" Herr Schneider moaned. Georgeanna pulled the vinyl curtain aside.

"Oh Lord," Georgeanna gasped. Herr Schneider was crumpled on the floor of the tub. Spray from the shower spigot pummeled him. Bright red blood streamed from a gash on his forehead and mixed with the water, so that he lay in a pink puddle. He attempted to pull himself up to a seated position and whimpered in pain.

"Hold still," Georgeanna said, turning off the faucet. Again, Herr Schneider attempted to sit up. He cried out and fell back into the bathtub. His cheek pressed against the porcelain edge, while his legs twisted in the opposite direction of his torso. His contorted figure was all bony angles and blue veiny tributaries threading across papier-mâché skin. He looked like one of her mom's worn washrags being wrung out in the kitchen sink. Georgeanna noticed a violet bruise, so dark it was almost black, blooming on Herr Schneider's hip where it jutted unnaturally toward the ceiling. Herr Schneider lifted a shaky hand and laid it across his groin.

Georgeanna yanked a bath towel from a hook just next to the tub and draped it over the old man's body. She hadn't been to medical school yet, but she'd worked with her dad enough to know that moving Herr Schneider before the emergency team arrived could make his injuries worse. She fished a washcloth from the bottom of the tub. The blood-tinged water soaked the cuff of her denim jacket, dying the stone-washed hem pale pink, the same color as the filleted bellies of trout sold at the market in the *Innenstadt*. She used the washcloth to wipe away blood from Herr Schneider's face where it had caked and clotted near his ear lobe, in the crease of his nose, and at the corner of his lips. She wondered if P.J. had been covered in blood the same way. She wondered if anyone had been there to clean it off of him.

■ ■ ■

Georgeanna's flight left Frankfurt at daybreak. She pressed her cheek against the plane's oval window as it flew above the sunrise's citrus beams—orange, lemon yellow, grapefruit pink —that streamed across the tops of clouds. Below she could see the ribbony, grey-blue twist of the Rhine, flowing with the same currents that had guided Herr Schneider's family all those years ago. She regretted she hadn't had the chance to tell him she was leaving, had just waved goodbye to the ambulance, red and blue lights flashing, as it rattled away over the cobblestone street. With just a few days warning, she hadn't been able to say goodbye to most anyone except for Birgit—not Alex or any of her other classmates, not the landlord who managed the dorm, or the German professor who repeated stories to her after class about his own study abroad in Ohio two decades ago. Deep down, she knew she wouldn't be back. She knew she'd wiring money to Birgit to mail the brown packing boxes home to Kentucky.

She also never had the chance to properly say goodbye to P.J. She'd hugged him before she left for the airport eight months ago, but that wasn't a real goodbye. What would she have said anyway? How do you say goodbye to your sixteen-year-old brother? A real goodbye. More than just a quick hug and a shoulder squeeze, or a playful headlock. More than just telling him to *Be good and have fun,* with its implied inferences to teenage mischief. How was she to know it was their last goodbye?

Georgeanna's mom had called the previous night to tell her that Trent would be picking her up at the airport, just as Georgeanna had assumed. He'd probably meet her at the gate, waiting for one of those airport hugs from the movies, when the woman throws her arms around the guy's neck, lifts her feet off the floor, and plants a long-lost lover's kiss on the guy's lips. Just thinking of it made her sick to her stomach—hugging Trent in the terminal, the musky smell of his collar pressed against her nose. She hated the thought of leaving the airport, hated thinking of chivalrous Trent carrying her half-packed suitcase. She hated thinking of the drive home on those same old roads with her same old boyfriend, only now without her brother at the other end, awaiting her arrival.

Tears, the same ones that kept popping out of nowhere these past few days, streamed down her cheeks and clouded her view of the Rhine that still wound between the green, brown, and grey-hued patchwork of the forests and towns below. Just a few days before she'd left for West Germany, Georgeanna sat with her dad on the bank of the creek in their back yard. "Did you know that all the water in the world is connected?" he'd asked her. "The water from this stream will someday be a part of the ocean. It'll make its way to the Cumberland River, then on to the Mississippi, all the way to the Gulf of Mexico."

Even though they'd been discussing the courses she still needed for medical school admission, Georgeanna nodded, accustomed to humoring her dad's random musings. He went on, "Even the rain originally came from the ocean, maybe once it was part of the Pacific or the Indian Ocean or a glacier in Alaska, and when you drink it, all that is in you. All of that becomes part of you."

"Sure, Dad. That's interesting," Georgeanna said, and then diverted their conversation back to her pre-med curriculum.

Who knew that not even a year later, medical school admission would be the furthest thing from her mind, that it would be her smallest worry, that she'd be flying home early to a family of four instead of five?

Georgeanna's tears dripped from her chin onto her chest and trickled down the V-neck of her blouse, where they pooled between her breasts. She didn't even try to wipe them away. She didn't care how red her eyes were, how wet her shirt was, how the other passengers and the stewardess stared at her curiously. As she cried she wondered where her tears would go if she never soaked them up with a tissue. They'd evaporate eventually, and when they did, would they course through the plane's ventilation system? Would they filter into a cloud, a fat cumulus cloud thick with moisture? According to her dad's logic, her tears would mix with all the water in the world. When that cloud became too heavy, her tears would rain back down to the earth. They would patter the clay-shingled roofs of the houses below, slip down the steep spire of the cathedral, get swept out of the way by a car's frantic windshield wipers, offer a satisfying splash to a little girl jumping into a curbside puddle. Maybe some of those tears would water a garden, or Herr Schneider's herbs. Maybe some would flow into the Rhine River where they'd mingle with the bitter tears of Lorelei and meld with the spilled blood of all those young sailors lured by the false promise of a sweet song. ■

WHAT MY BROTHER'S BROWNNESS MEANS TO HIM

Nothing. As in no
preference for the thick Persian

stews that grew him tall.
As in no scars from my mother—scared

of the English words convulsing in her Farsi
throat—how she'd heave

screams of *you're stupid* at us just for being
something she had created.

My brother and I are the only members of our family
who share the same shade of brown—that's how

it can happen. My dad sees us as white,

he didn't see my sister starving.
Most people don't have good vision—

a friend recently said that I'm *white
as fuck.* Here's a brown education on being

American: my mother spoons food to punish
her mouth in front of the fridge

until she sees the bottom of the plastic
containers every time we return home.

My brother calls our mother *foreign*

when people ask him to explain his existence.
See how my mother shrinks in front of men

the silence she tends to carefully as a bruise,
the warmth of my nephew's hand

as his legs shutter from a gunshot to the head.
My brother joined the Navy to choose his exit

wounds. This country doesn't convulse
when a brown boy dies. Nothing.

NATASHA PEPPERL

ON THE MEN OF THIS FAMILY: TO THEIR FUTURE LOVERS

These men are West Virginia pickaxe, fluent
        in uprooting and the duration of heat
    before a harvest. How hands can dance
along to an old folk tune crooning of betrayal.
        Meaning don't yell or else
    they'll go south bouncing like loose change.

For they, too, are the glint of hardened clay and salt
        on the brow. Go ahead and rest
    your head on those rocky shoulders come home
after a day's hard work. Meaning root with your cheek
        until you find the soft spot of flesh
    between tendons and be greeted by the day's sheen.

What I mean to say is, collect your warmth

before you learn how Septembers spread to deliver stillborns
        and leaves crumble to be lost, a fluency in pondering
blood under fingernails and lighted living rooms.
Meaning, these men know their ghosts
        by name: a buried father who wrote their mother *you are my flower*
        in the sidewalk crack—and a nephew they watched swell in his death.

What I mean to say is, after the second murder

my man plants a red apple
        tree as a sign of hope. His body tense
as he strikes pickaxe against the earth—all her heavenless things
glinting in the sun on the run before a buck scapes his rooting antlers against
the wispy trunk and teeths the leaves. The men respond with a hedge
of wire. But come spring, the tree's buds are met with ice—and unfurl in scars.

NATASHA PEPPERL

FIRST GRADE AUTOBIOGRAPHY

After Donika Kelly's "Fourth Grade Autobiography"

We live in Montgomery, Alabama.
Our backyard is crowned
with a prehistoric tree
wrapped in vines.

My favorite things:
brother, that monstrous
tree, and dad towing us
on his bike. We marvel
up hills, at his muscles.

Once mom screams she's lost
our baby sister, who turns up
swallowed by greenery and dark
of under the deck.

We don't believe in Santa, we
don't believe in monsters.
We believe the devil hungers
to steal our tender hearts.

Everything swarms

of humidity and cockroaches
and mosquitos. I slap my legs
and watch blood run in tears.

Once my brother and I build air
balloons with black trash
bags and laundry vent
exhales to float
beyond our tree.

We are too young to name
escape, or its roots
or the berries of our other
tree—how they kiss
our teeth.

NATASHA PEPPERL

AN EXCERPT FROM

KIN: A MEMOIR

SHAWNA KAY RODENBERG

Grand Marais, Minnesota, 1978-1979

Most mornings, the first sound I heard was either a mosquito, tinny in my ear, or the rusty springs of the rough-hewn door as it closed behind my father when he left to stoke the stoves in the other buildings or to wait tables in town. The second sound was my sister's easy breath. She fell asleep rubbing my mousy, fine hair between her fingers, a process she called fuzzying, so before I could move, I had to loosen her chubby toddler fingers from the tangled loops of my hair, and I did this as carefully as if I were untying a knot in a thin gold necklace, so she would keep sleeping.

In Grand Marais, Minnesota, there were only a few weeks in summer when a fire in the stove was unnecessary. My father kept ours packed with wood and poked the coals regularly, but some mornings the heat seemed feeble against the cold, since the bare plywood walls of our room in the Bunk House were uninsulated, and I had to will myself to leave the pocket of warmth trapped beneath the heavy quilts. It felt like leaping into the northern shore of Lake Superior, which was just across the road and vast as an ocean, but visible only in winter when all but the pine trees were bare...

The four of us shared half of the Bunk House, which was about the size and length of a singlewide trailer, and sometimes my mother divided it further by using an old bedsheet as a curtain, so she and Dad could have privacy. Despite our small living space, we weren't terribly crowded because we didn't have many possessions: *Lay not up for yourselves treasures upon earth, where moth and rust doth corrupt.* The Bible was clear that people who collected too much stuff on earth were idol-worshippers, in love with the carnal world and at best only halfway committed to the Kingdom of God. Misti and I had no toys or dolls because they were essentially idols, graven images. My mother disagreed with this idea because she thought little girls needed to practice if they were ever going to learn biblical woman- and motherhood, and I wholeheartedly agreed with her, but she said so only in private.

I did have my complete set of the *Little House on the Prairie* series, which she chose for my birthday, a special edition so the spines and matching cardboard case were baby blue instead of buttery yellow like the ones at the library. Dad made the gift even more special by hanging a small wooden shelf above my side of the bed I shared with Misti, and the matching set of books complete in their case on my very own shelf was my most prized possession.

I never tired of reading those books, especially *Little House in the Big Woods*, because no matter which chapter I chose, I could see myself in the story. Laura Ingalls lived in the wilderness and, though she loved her father best, found being good impossible. Jealous of her sister's golden hair, Laura smacked her across the face hard and had to be spanked. She loved sugar and spoke out of turn. She played tricks on people who treated her badly because she was poor. She embarrassed herself by hoarding pebbles from the shores of Lake Pepin, tearing the pocket of her dress. I didn't tell anybody, but I thought about her like she was my best friend.

And just like her, I was happy to play with wood chips and thimbles, thrilled to receive simple tokens for birthdays or Christmas, which, like all holidays, we were not supposed to celebrate, though each year my mother conspired to create our own secret Christmas celebration together. In the few private moments we had between our schedule of meals and women's Bible study, school, which was more Bible study, chores, and evening services, she'd gather Misti and me on her bed and retrieve a handful of treasures from the back of her drawer, tucked carefully behind her clothes. She'd pass the bright Christmas tin of peanut butter candy and pinwheels my grandmother sent and watch Misti and me gobble them down. Then, while we ate, she'd work her way through the small stack of cards, pointing out the fancy foil sticker seals on the envelopes, reading the addresses aloud, and asking me to guess who sent each card more than a thousand miles to us.

■ ■ ■

During free time there were a few places I liked to go.
There was a small wooden sandbox next to the school, and
Misti played there while I checked my secret hiding spot,
a nook I constructed by propping a small board against a
covered corner of the sandbox. It was a holding tank for any
special rocks or other treasures that I found but wasn't quite
ready to commit to my collection, and any turtles, frogs, or
moths I kept until they managed to escape.

Then there was the creek, cold as ice water, and though I
loved to play in it, I was not allowed to get my clothes wet, and
my hands went numb if I spent too much time sifting through
the rocks and sticks that settled there. So, after we played in
the creek, I dragged Misti across the yard to the green- house
of buckled lumber and clear plastic, to warm our hands. I
loved the bitter tomato plant smell inside, and the way that,
no matter how cold the day, the air inside the greenhouse
was always warm and balmy. It was a small space though, and
Misti got impatient being stuck inside, so we wandered to
the swings, where I pushed her until Mom came to find us,
to take us back to our room and get cleaned up for supper
and the evening service. She combed her hair and ours and
changed our clothes for cleaner ones when they were soiled.
She gathered the things she used during church and I did the
same, mimicking her in every way I was able, gathering my
baggie of markers and a fresh stack of paper in case I would be
allowed to draw.

Eventually, I would also bring along my half-size guitar,
another birthday present, which Dad took me all the way to
Duluth to buy. He told me to choose the finish and even a
strap, so I could stand and play during praise services. I chose
a deep caramel finish and a bright blue strap in a pattern like

the edge of an Indian blanket. Our school had made a field trip to the nearby Grand Portage Indian Reservation for a demonstration of old arts, where Chippewa women wove blankets and worked deer hides with stones and men hollowed logs into canoes and pressed the hides around tipis. When we were there, I played a game in my mind where I was a pioneer girl, lost among the Indians, combing the dirt for colorful beads that might have been left behind, like Laura had when she and her Pa stumbled on an abandoned Indian camp.

Back inside the Tabernacle, Peter was already being fed, but the smell of beef liver filled the air and made me feel sick even before it was plunked steaming and swelling onto my plate. When we sat together at the table, Dad said liver was a rare treat and nudged me to eat it. I gagged. He skewered a piece on a fork and pressed it toward my mouth. I gagged again. He put ketchup on it, hoping to hide the taste. I felt guilty and tried to bring a forkful to my mouth but gagged again. He grabbed me by the shoulder for a cursory trip to the outhouse, where he reminded me to be thankful for what I had and spanked me with his flat, open hand.

The smell of beef liver filled the air and made me feel sick even before it was plunked steaming and swelling onto my plate.

He wasn't too angry, and the spanking wasn't very hard, a small price to pay for not having to swallow the fibrous, netted flesh or the slimy worms of onions surrounding it, all dripping in blood juice. By the time we walked back to the table, Mom had removed the plate, so I wouldn't have to try again. Dad said he was going to take a walk, and she pushed a buttered roll into my hand under the table. There was a dessert, and before he left, Dad said I shouldn't have any, but though Mom agreed with him and said I should listen, I could tell by the easy nod she gave him that she'd helped make the dessert, a simple vanilla custard, and set a dish back for me.

For the last time of the day, the tables were packed away and the folding chairs arranged, this time into rows with an aisle down the center. One of the men lugged a heavy wooden pulpit to the front of the room as the grown-ups milled around and caught up with each other. Mom unfolded a small blanket on the floor in front of her chair and gave Misti a board book, so familiar it no longer held any magic. Still, my sister kept quiet and fell asleep every night before the service was over.

The services followed a loose pattern. They were always led by an elder and opened with a prayer and extended Spirit-filled praise service, where all the adults spoke in tongues, which I thought, even though I did it, too, sounded like baby talk, and I had to be careful not to giggle about it. While the adults' hands were lifted and their eyes were closed, I peeked around, especially fascinated by one woman who always stomped her foot while she repeated *Shalalabubububah* over and over again.

Between sets of songs and tongues, when hands were lowered and quiet filled the room, prophecies and visions were shared. The visions were passed forward on slips of paper and read to the room, and the prophecies were spoken aloud, spontaneously, and all began with *Yea*. Both were full of familiar signs and symbols: *I saw complete darkness everywhere I looked. Suddenly there was an eruption in the sky and it opened up. Much light appeared and it formed like a crown. It looked like the crown you see on the Statue of Liberty. I then heard the word Liberty.* Mom had the gift of both visions and prophecy, regularly jotting down the things she saw on slips of paper and handing them to me to pass forward.

I liked trying to guess which were hers when they were read aloud, which wasn't very difficult, because hers always contained chains, flowers, witches, and swans, not the dumb statues and kitchen appliances in some of the others.

The praise services got rowdy. Several people played guitars and tambourines. When I brought my guitar, I used a notebook Dad put together for me, where he wrote out the chords for many of the songs we sang. When I played well, he let me know by raising his eyebrows at me and sometimes squeezing my shoulder.

When the praise service ended, usually about the time we all felt tired, it was time for the teaching, usually given by the elders, and on rare occasions by traveling ministry, even by Brother Sam via the same cassette tapes of recorded sermons and Bible studies we listened to in our rooms at night on battery-powered tape players. Some of Brother Sam's sermons were difficult to fall asleep to, because they were lists of the many prophecies of Revelations that had already come to pass in the End Times where we found ourselves. His sermons made me worry about my grandparents back in Kentucky. Were they too worldly? Had they sacrificed enough? Grandpa Roy refused to go to church. It seemed impossible, but the sermons were often terrifying and boring at the same time.

What I found most impossible was sitting still for hours, listening to one person, any person, talk. By the end of the day, even though I had played outside and explored the creek, even though I did not mind school or Bible study, I felt like I had already spent hours sitting in a hard metal chair, trying to keep my legs from swinging, to avoid making unnecessary racket by rustling the pages in my Bible or dropping something loud against the floor. During evening services, I felt so bored I could hardly concentrate, and tried to put off asking to use the bathroom long enough that Dad might nod in permission. The slow walk from my chair to the outhouse and then back felt like a little recess.

To distract myself in the meantime, I often read my red birthday Bible or studied one of the illustrations inside, memorizing all the details in the picture. My favorites were the ones with women, *Abraham, Isaac,* and *Sarah; Rebekah at the Well; Manna from Heaven; Gifts for the Tabernacle;* the *Birth of Jesus;* and *Jairus's Daughter Healed.*

I had flipped through the pictures hundreds of times and knew them all by heart, especially the coins and symbols in the back, the bronze lepton, or "widow's mite," the Ethiopian's chariot. When we traveled to Body conventions, where we could disappear into a crowd of hundreds of people, I was allowed to draw and make crafts during sermons, but in Grand Marais Dad was quite a bit stricter. Drawing meant I couldn't pay attention, and how else was I supposed to learn discipline and self-control?

I flipped to the book of Judges where I knew I'd find the story of Jael, one of my favorites, when Deborah, the warrior woman and judge, advised the military commander Barak to go to battle against King Jabin, but Barak was scared and asked her to come along. Because of his lack of faith, Deborah prophesied that Jabin's army would be defeated once and for all, but by a woman instead of by soldiers.

The two armies battled on the plains, divinely flooded by torrential rain and the overflowing Wadi Kishon; the brutal soldiers of Jabin's army lost ground as their horses and heavy iron chariots became mired in an endless sea of mud. The terrified leader of Jabin's army, Sisera, fled the battlefield and found himself in the neighboring camp of the Kenites, knocking at the tent of Jael. Jael had to have been terrified coming face-to-face with her bloody, battle-crazed tormentor, but she welcomed him inside and cared for him. She covered him with a blanket and gave him clean fresh milk to drink. But she must have put something in the milk, because Sisera fell into such a deep sleep that he did not wake when she used a stone mallet to drive a tent stake, the only weapon she had, through his temple and into the ground below. The battle was won and she became a hero, immortalized in song: *Extolled above women be Jael, extolled above women in the tent. He asked for water, she gave him milk; She brought him cream in a lordly dish.*

It seemed miraculous to me, two women defeating an army of men, Deborah with her wisdom and Jael with her might. And it seemed even more miraculous that I, thousands of years later, was reading the lyrics of Deborah's Song, the same song that Jael and the Israelites sung in the camps that night while dancing around their fires. I felt proud that my mother was named for Deborah.

After I finished the story, I checked in to see how much time had passed, but Misti was still awake and my father was highlighting passages in his Bible, which meant we had at least an hour to go. I asked to go to the bathroom, but he shook his head no. It was too soon. So I asked if I could use my markers to draw, and he nodded, visibly disappointed in me. Around the room the other kids were quiet and content, perfectly still in their seats.

Then I had an idea. Instead of drawing, I would use the markers to highlight my Bible like my father did. I knew he would be proud to see me paying attention, focused on the Word. I flipped to random pages and ran my markers over passages, my face thoughtful and contemplative like his. I switched out the markers to color-code different passages, also like him. It felt like important grown-up work.

The rest of the service passed quickly. Misti was sound asleep by the time we sang the final song of the night. But when I looked over at my father who was watching me, his face was unhappy and confused. My stomach knotted up, and the skin on my neck felt electric, like an alarm going off. As the service ended, the adults took their time bidding each other good night, but Dad told Mom he was taking me back to the room. She asked if everything was okay, and he said he'd explain later.

We walked in silence back to the Bunk House, but I was still hopeful. I couldn't think of anything I'd done wrong. I thought maybe I had made too much noise when I was highlighting, preoccupied with the work. His face was like a barricade between us, like a moat. I asked him what happened, but he didn't answer. The closer we got to our door, the more panicked I felt, as it dawned on me what was about to happen.

No, Daddy, no. Please, no. I cried quietly, looking behind me. I knew if I made a scene, it would only embarrass him and make everything worse.

He ignored me, but when we were back in the room, he asked to see my Bible and I showed him, falling all over myself, shifting from foot to foot, talking quickly in stutters, practically hyperventilating as I tried to explain that I was doing what he does, highlighting passages, paying attention. He asked which passages I chose and why, and I drew a blank, struck dumb, stupefied with fear. He asked again, *How did you choose the passages you highlighted?* and pointed out one place where I used my dark purple marker, showing me how the verses beneath were illegible beneath the inky block I had carelessly, irreverently filled in.

That was when I realized I had ruined my first Bible, the one he let me choose in Duluth. Just as we had with my guitar, he made a special trip for it. From all the stacks of Bibles, he let me select the one I wanted, and a zippered case to match. He even bought me lunch while we were there, fresh salty fish pulled from Lake Superior—big fish, not the tiny fried smelt we ate all the time, which were hauled in by the men with nets and buckets. In Duluth we ate on a restaurant porch that looked out over the water, then walked together along the water's edge in a park full of flowers and pine needles.

He had trusted me with my own copy of the Bible, and I ruined it. I knew I would never have done the same to my *Little House* books. The horror of my mistake began to sink in. *I'm sorry, Daddy. I won't do it ever again. I promise, I promise.* When I panicked, I couldn't think straight and said the same things over and over again. I couldn't beg fast enough.

Usually he used his belt, unbuckling it and jerking it through the loops of his pants in one snapping motion, but this time he was so angry he grabbed the butterfly-shaped flyswatter we used to kill mosquitoes. The swatter whistled through the air like a swarm of wasps descending, covering my lower back, behind, and legs, occasionally stinging other

He had trusted me with my own copy of the Bible, and I had ruined it. I knew I would never have done the same to my Little House *books.*

places, a shoulder, an elbow, as I jumped and danced around him, trying to block the stings with my hands and the backs of my arms.

My mother stepped on a wasp nest when she was only twelve, the year her father died, and I thought it probably felt the same. She'd told me the story dozens of times, how her eyes swelled shut and her own mother and aunties swaddled her in creek mud and rags. The mud cooled the stings and drew out the venom, and she lay like that for days, with only her nose and mouth exposed, so she could breathe. When the swelling finally went down and they undid the cocoon of her, she had started her period. The stings had scared her young body into womanhood. She hadn't been ready, but then, she said, no one ever is.

With each swat, he said a word, like the stings were punctuation. *How. Can. You. Do. This.* I felt so sweaty I wondered if the wetness I felt on my skin was blood, though of course it wasn't. I wondered if I would start my period or pee on myself, the most embarrassing thing, so I held my privates with one hand and tried to block the stings with the other.

When I looked up at him, he was sweating, too. I started to count silently, inside my head, because sometimes that helped the time pass. Eventually I stopped paying attention and balled up on the floor. Instead of the stings, I thought about Jael and Deborah, about thomsonite, and about my mother, how I wanted her with me.

When he was finished, he sat on the floor next to me. I thought I smelled pee, but I checked and I hadn't wet myself. Exhausted, he reached over to pull me into his lap, a puddle of tears, and we were both crying. He told me he was sorry, and that he hated having to whip me. He said it was the hardest thing, disciplining a child, and he should never do it when he was angry. He was going to work on that. He said this was how God must have felt watching Jesus be whipped, and that he knew I didn't mean to do what I did, he only whipped me because he loved me, it was all for my own good.

I nestled deeper into his arms, my relief bordering on bliss. After a whipping, he was softer than at any other time. He touched my face and told me he loved me. It felt like a fresh start, and I promised myself and him that I would try harder to behave, to listen more closely to my conscience, which he said would guide me.

But there was another feeling, too, small and hard in my chest, that I tried to ignore as I soaked up the flood of his affection, a feeling like the one I had for Peter, when I gave him a drink of water and stared into his eyes. I tried to push it out of my mind, to pretend it wasn't there as Dad cradled me, rocking me while I cried, my breath catching like hiccups. It was a feeling I didn't want to have, so wicked I thought it might kill me if I let it grow inside my heart. I was afraid the tenderness I felt for my dad would disappear, and I would be left with only the one feeling, a question really: *Why are you like this?*

Mom pushed through the door carrying Misti and looked at me and Dad as she walked through the room to lay my sister, still sound asleep, carefully on the bed. I felt overwhelming relief—the discipline was finished, my sister was sleeping, my mother was with me again. My relief turned to happiness, and I wondered if I might even have time to read my books. I was often allowed to stay up a little later after a particularly bad whipping.

Mom pulled me from Dad's arms, walked me to the bed, and undressed me, touching the bright red butterflies blooming on my skin with the soft pads of her fingers. She dampened a washrag with some of the cool water from our jug and pressed it against each winged welt. She changed my panties and pulled my nightgown over my head. "What happened, Shawna Kay?" she asked.

I told her about the Bible and said I was sorry. She didn't comment on the punishment or my mistake, just tucked me into bed, worry covering her face like a veil. I wondered what she was thinking, because that scared me more than the whippings, that she might also be angry with me and decide I was too much trouble. She might wash her hands of me, leaving me alone in a world full of people who felt like strangers no matter how much time I spent with them. I loved Misti, but she was an easy puzzle I had to solve every day, and

Dad was as unpredictable and distant as the God of the Old Testament. Without my mother, I would be truly alone.

She kissed my cheek and pulled the covers up to my shoulders, laying her head briefly on the pillow next to mine so we could stare at each other. After a minute or two she made a silly face, and in spite of myself, I smiled.

Dad was in the next room getting ready for bed, lighting our oil lamp with its colored kerosene. He put a tape into the tape player, but instead of Brother Sam's voice, it was Ann Kinsley's, a woman from The Body we all loved to listen to, her voice ringing clearly through pretty old hymns, the same ones my Grandma Betty loved, like "Blessed Assurance." Dad chose the tape for me, so I could fall asleep to my favorite songs. Mom nodded over her shoulder, pointing out what he was doing and how sorry he was. She wanted me to forgive him.

He called her name and she rose and left, pulling the sheet curtain behind her. ∎

SHAWNA KAY RODENBERG

There's a certain amount of defiance hovering between Shawna Kay Rodenberg's words as she discusses *Kin*, her debut memoir slated for publication by Bloomsbury in June—and after spending time with her searching, resilient book, it is easy to understand why. *Kin* recounts her family's exile from their native Eastern Kentucky to rural Minnesota, where Rodenberg spent much of her childhood as a member of The Body, a Christian fundamentalist End Times commune that preached a strict, patriarchal gospel of denial and austerity. When the family abandoned the group to return to Appalachia, they were left to reckon with the effects of The Body on their family and to confront the fraught, sometimes violent dynamics playing out within the confines of their home—the legacy of Vietnam and generations of hardship and abuse. The volatile relationship between Rodenberg and her father occupies the heart of the memoir, and it is her search for empathy and understanding—of her father, of her family, of Appalachia, of herself—that drives the fractured narrative.

"My family's story is epic," Rodenberg declared in a recent conversation with *Appalachian Review*, "and I'm proud of who we are and everything we've survived."

■ ■ ■

JASON KYLE HOWARD: *Kin* **recounts how, when you were a child, your family left Eastern Kentucky to join an End Times religious community in rural Minnesota—and the lingering effects of that experience after your family eventually left. Where did the book begin for you? How did you come to write it?**

SHAWNA KAY RODENBERG: My dear friend and mentor, Mark Wunderlich, whom I met when I was studying poetry as an MFA candidate at the Bennington Writing Seminars, suggested that some of my poems were bogged down by too much narrative burden, and that maybe I should write a memoir, which was the absolute last thing I ever wanted to do. I had chosen to study poetry for many reasons, but most of all I think because of its inscrutable and mysterious nature, which felt like a kind of protective veil one could

Shawna Kay Rodenberg

hide behind, if she wanted to. I think many writers become writers because they long to be known from a safe distance, and I know that's true for me. "Just write it like no one will ever read it," Mark said, "like you're writing something for your kids to read after you're gone." A year and a half later I had what I thought might be a prologue, which I showed to another professor at Bennington, Ben Anastas, who teaches creative nonfiction, and like Mark, he believed in the book right away, long before I did, and helped me machete my way through the high weeds of the first few chapters until I could see a possible path.

JKH: A major focus of the book is the fear and violence that existed inside your home and was centered on your father. At one point you describe his decision to not become a coal miner in Eastern Kentucky: "He said the men there lived most of their lives underground, and that it hardened them. He had tried to make a different kind of life." This passage seems to be symbolic of something beyond his career path. What else was he running from?

SKR: My dad rarely talked about his dad and the mines, so when he did, I paid especially close attention and decided to include a few of those moments in *Kin* because I believe they point to a fairly universal experience. I'm speaking about the way my family and most families in marginalized communities and regions become preoccupied with the effort required to bear up beneath heavy traumatic lineages and psychic burdens, the struggle to carry on from whatever place in the generational relay race you're passed the family baton. From an early age, I sensed that the conflict in my family was an old one that existed long before I made my way into the world. I also sensed that many of the families around mine bore the same or heavier burdens—sometimes I witnessed those burdens firsthand. To his credit, my dad was always extraordinarily open with me about the ways his burdens affected our relationship. Later, as an adult, I was humbled and pained to find that my burdens affected my relationships with my own children, too. The thing is, every generation does a little better, because each learns from the mistakes of the previous one and starts a little fresher and further along in the relay race. And, though I wouldn't want to speak for my dad, since only he can truly know where he was and is coming from, I think we're all only ever running from ourselves. At least, that's true for me.

JKH: In the prologue you write, "I know from experience that the price of letting your version of a story exist anywhere outside your own head is that the moment you do it's no longer your version but public property, subject to scrutiny and denial, and impossible to control." A couple of things strike me about that passage. First, you are acknowledging the inherent subjectivity of memoir—that *Kin* **is your truth, "your version of a story" as only you can tell it. Were you aware of when your memory of an event or situation didn't align with those of others? If so, how did you handle approaching that material?**

SKR: When you grow up in a storytelling family like I did, you notice right away that some stories overlap, and that different storytellers remember the details of events and the characteristics of people differently, sometimes in ways that seem completely contradictory. This might be because of the way they were feeling on any given day, or because they weren't as invested in an event and didn't sense its significance at the time. It might be because of water under the generational bridge, so to speak, which means biases and prejudices, that we always feel more loyalty toward some family members than others. Often, we're distracted by our own personal drama, so we miss things, or we're chicken about conflict, so we make ourselves scarce whenever there is one. Writing a memoir forces you to interrogate your memory, but also to confront how much you don't remember. It reveals how many different versions of his/her/their life anyone could write, and how often the psyche, especially under duress, can't resist filling in the blanks. I would hope that any loved one whose versions of our shared experiences differ from my own would give me the benefit of the doubt, believing that my heart was in the right place and I worked to be honest and fair in my treatment of everyone whose stories overlapped with and altered my own. My family's story is epic, and I'm proud of who we are and everything we've survived. I believe we deserve our place in American literature, that our story is worth telling and reading and reflecting on. I hope that belief is apparent to anyone who reads *Kin*.

JKH: As a follow-up, the memoir goes to some tough places—not only about your family, but also about the region, particularly the streak of machismo that runs through Appalachia and is sometimes aggressive and violent. Are you nervous about how the book will be received by your family and community? How have you prepared yourself?

SKR: I think what Appalachia is working out is less a streak of machismo and more a foundational matrix of Bible-based patriarchy—which is also true for the country-at-large as is evidenced by the political turmoil of the last several years. Patriarchy might be more visible in Appalachia, where, for example, women might fix their husbands' plates before they eat, but we know that household chores and child rearing fall disproportionately to women throughout America, even in households where women are the primary breadwinners. Truly, as my book details, I've never been good at submitting to patriarchy, and of course, that always meant conflict, though I want to be clear that I don't think the problem is men (because patriarchy actually stinks for them, too) but a terrible imbalance of power which I refuse to acknowledge as sustainable or healthy. All of this is to say that from the very first days of writing *Kin*, I knew there would be backlash, because it's only an extension, the latest iteration of the fight I, and I believe many other American women, were born fighting. I choose to believe that any backlash is only confirmation of the book's value in that fight, that it's doing good things in the world.

JKH: Religious fundamentalism, poverty, abuse and misogyny exist everywhere, but they are often applied to Appalachia as stereotypes. As a memoirist, do you think you can write about those issues without contributing to stereotypical perceptions of the region?

SKR: This question worried me to death as I was writing *Kin*. First, I think it's important to remember, if only for sanity's sake, that my primary task was to tell my own story, not to represent the whole of Appalachia and the 25 million people who live there, each with a story as unique and as common as my own. And, secondly, I think it's important to say that religious fundamentalism, poverty, abuse, and misogyny are not Appalachian traits, but the inevitable products of late-stage extractive capitalism, underregulated commercial greed, abandonment by corrupt governments, wobbly, dilapidated infrastructures, and exploitative, bootstrap theologies. So, since I've been given a voice that carries a bit, it's my responsibility to be honest about how hard it can be to grow up in a place that might be one of the most dramatic, visible examples of the failures of all those outdated modes of governance. For better or worse, America's industrial development was fueled by coal extracted from my parents', grandparents', and great-grandparents' land. For better or worse, coal fed the engines of American expansion. Yes, coal as an industry is over, but coal is more than industry in Appalachia; it's identity, too, and it has to be replaced with something. It's politically irresponsible to leave an entire region hanging for decades just because there's nothing else they have that you want. And pretending that everything is okay lets the wrong people off the hook.

JKH: One thing that struck me both as I was reading the book and then after I finished it was how, after recounting numerous instances of emotionally and physically violent behavior from your father—and the lack of determined intervention from your mother—you managed to find a reservoir of empathy for both of them and for other family members. Where did that come from? Was that impulse present on the page from the beginning, or was it something you had to work towards?

SKR: One of my earliest memories is of going to a drive-in movie called *Savannah Smiles,* a cheesy little tearjerker about some criminals who kidnap a little girl for ransom but come to love her, give her back to her parents, and face going to jail. I cried so hard for days after seeing that movie that my mom was worried about me, mostly because I couldn't stand that the kidnappers wouldn't be able to see the little girl again, that the world didn't work that way because nobody cared that loving someone had changed them for the better, and I've really always been that way. Sometimes it has meant that people assume I'm not very smart, because I value mercy over justice, so I let things go and try to understand and see the best in people. Maybe because I've needed so much of it, I don't want to live in a world where mercy isn't the driving force. Nick Flynn's *Another Bullshit Night in Suck City* was the first merciful memoir I read and thought, primarily because of his loving treatment of his father, "Maybe I *could* bear writing my story down."

JKH: I'm always deeply intrigued by how books are structured and how those choices can be connected to themes and meaning. *Kin* moves back and forth in time, sometimes alternating in focus on different characters. How did you arrive at this structure, and how do you think it contributes to the book's meaning?

SKR: At first, I thought I would write the chapters focused on my own story in present tense, and the family stories in past tense, but about halfway through the project I realized that wasn't necessary, and that in fact I liked the effect of blending my stories and the stories of the women who came before me, who shared so many of the same experiences coming of age in Eastern Kentucky. In the earliest moments of the book, I knew that I wanted the first half of *Kin*, the stranger-in-a-strange-land chapters, to be annotated and contextualized by stories my mother shared with me dozens of times, but once I made it to the second part of the book and our return to Letcher County, it became clear that the remainder of my story had to parallel my dad's. As teenagers, we both had fraught relationships with our fathers. We both rebelled.

We both suffered, sometimes from without and sometimes within. And, we left. Honestly, the inclusion of family stories that shaped my own felt more like an ethical decision than a stylistic one. I didn't see any other way to be fair and truthful.

JKH: So much of the harmful behavior you write about is centered on religion and misogyny—and how the two can be intertwined. You write about how The Body subjugated women, how you were abused by a member of the community, how your family made hard sacrifices to remain members. How, even after your family left, the influence of The Body remained. I'm thinking of how you hid rock cassette tapes from your dad and you were even the focus of an exorcism. Yet you also describe the community as a place where solidarity and tenderness could exist, particularly among the women. This left me wondering where you stand with religion and belief today.

SKR: Well, technically I'm a Catholic, because I converted when I remarried in 2000. It seemed such a gorgeous religion to me, though my husband, having grown up in it, is fairly ambivalent. But, right away, I loved all the sacramentals that evangelicals deem idolatrous—the statuary, stained glass, and candles, the incense and the practiced gesturing, and as someone who spent hours at a time in church conventions and revivals and Bible studies, I find it kind of endearing when Catholics complain about an hour-long Mass. Because I'm a progressive feminist who believes in reproductive freedom and sexual expression, I do struggle with parts of the doctrine, especially the supernatural bits, the demons and miracles, but sometimes I just like the feeling of being in church. I think religion will always be an inclination of mine and the lens through which I view most of the American experience. I follow fundamentalist Instagrammers, bloggers, and conservative stay-at-home homeschooling mothers on YouTube, mostly I think because I like knowing what they're all up to, but sometimes because, admittedly, I find the language of the church as comforting as a weighted blanket. I have these periodic, intermittent obsessive periods with new religions, philosophies, even health and fitness. Ascetism is not an uncomfortable challenge for me, and I can turn literally anything into a religious practice.

JKH: Any memoir coming out today that is centered on Appalachia has to reckon with the spectre of *Hillbilly Elegy*, which was not received well among the Appalachian literary community due to a number of factors, including a lack of nuance and sweeping generalizations that were made about the region. Did that book, and the response to it, affect how you approached *Kin*?

SKR: I felt a little self-conscious about my primary issues with Vance's book, because I wasn't nearly as bothered that it was largely "negative" as I was that it was didactic, politically motivated, and easy. I have been scared that people might compare my book with *Hillbilly Elegy* because what I write doesn't always paint the most flattering picture. But, flattery is, by definition, insincere and deceitful, and I hope my readers will see that I very sincerely love and feel loyalty to the Kentucky mountains and the people who live there, the true beauty of both. Sadly, the thinly-veiled conservative bias of Vance's book predictably shifted the blame for Appalachia's struggles (poverty, drug abuse) onto the wrong shoulders. On the other hand, it did prime the pump for a greater Appalachian presence in mainstream American book culture, and it also taught many of my progressive, writerly, coastal-born friends a good lesson, since many of them initially loved it, revealing a great deal about their own naïve, neoliberal politics and shamefully limited understanding of rural America.

JKH: How were you changed by writing *Kin*?

SKR: That's a long list. Taking control of the narrative of my lived life, recreating the scenes that seemed most relevant and omitting those that weren't, or that I simply didn't want to share, empowered me in a way I hadn't anticipated. Telling the truth so publicly about who I am and what I believe has been liberating but also so terrifying that I'm glad I didn't realize what I was tackling when I started. Before writing *Kin* I thought I knew something about the personal cost of memoir, but I was clueless about the courage and endurance required to finish one. Following my younger selves (and my father's and mother's and grandmothers') through some of the darkest ravines of our shared story helped me love myself and my family, genuinely so, more than I thought possible. My mother died in October of 2018, and the solid, unyielding chore of the book carried me through the last years of her illness, her death, and the darkest moments of my grief in the ensuing years. I spent more than five years writing *Kin*, more than a decade if you count the narrative poems that would eventually become memoir chapters, so the process never really felt cathartic, but the mindful preservation of my own history has given me a sense at times of having been made whole again, or of things being "set to rights," as my mom used to say. Mostly, I'm just grateful every day that I get to be a writer, which feels like a dream. ∎

HIDE AND SEEK

It was the summer before
Uncle Bradley crashed his car
in the locust tree, the time of night
when children long to be seen.
Cigarettes embered in the yard like
lightning bugs, and the last warm swallows
of beer sloshed in bottoms of cans.
My aunts and uncles had all
abandoned the game while I waited,
concealed in the shortest maple
where I'd fled, feet flapping
the dewey grass. Then, behind leaves
with veins like back of my hand,
I heard a rustling and Brad's face
rose to me, fringed by his jangly blonde curls.
Twenty-three, the family's youngest
save me, he grinned into the kingdom
where my spine pressed to bark and my arms
rested on limbs as a throne. I accepted
his generous terms, the honor
of being found, and passed through
his warm hands to the ground.

JIMMY LONG

ANDROCZI'S WINE

He decanted a capful of gold
honey mead in the beveled sherry glass
mother reached from top shelves.
I remember it sparkled like his eyes
under an Alpine fedora. I can see
his creased cheeks. He'd been my age
when he fled the boys' Hungarian work camp
and hid under a chicken coop's floor boards,
his heartbeat defying their pecks. Finally,
the State busted him here, at our county fair,

cops dumping the sample-sized plastic
cups off his card table when a band
of middle school boys got buzzed.
They'd snickered and downed his finest
dandelion wine, that musk he crafted
from West Virginia weeds. What remained,
between quilter and apple butter vendor:
only a barn's dirt floor, a space where
something delicious he'd share with all
the world for free had been seized.

JIMMY LONG

THE LOST AND FOUND MUSEUM

LAURA MARSHALL

I was setting up the display for Halloween on the day the girl turned up, the eyes of the dolls staring at me—or maybe just past me—as I straightened them. It wasn't Halloween season proper, really, but a vague, humid autumn that we don't feel this far soouth, indicated by uncarved pumpkins and plastic yellow leaves rather than cooler weather. The dolls and animals are the largest part of my section at the museum; rows of shelves reaching the barn ceiling are filled with them, close to two hundred. Most of the animals are tattered and worn, missing tails or eyes or ears, and most of the dolls of the plastic infant variety feature half-closed eyes revealing tufts of missing eyelashes. There are three other dolls with cracked porcelain faces and delicate lace and velvet dresses, and frayed but shining curls. They look like they got off of the wrong bus.

In front of them is a three-foot high wooden house with a miniature wooden table and chairs and a plaid couch. Its surfaces are adorned with scaled-down plates and cups and a cuckoo clock. I have to take some of the lost animals or dolls and display them in the house, seated at the table having tea (or whiskey, I sometimes imagine) or painted plastic cookies. I change the scene each week, alternating out a family of bears for one of rabbits or dogs. Then I decorate the display for holidays. Plastic autumn now, and soon a foot-tall Christmas tree in the corner.

It's busy enough that we could probably do without the shtick. Not many people were visiting for that display, except for a few passing tourists with children that lost their toys at roadside restaurants, animals with unpaved highway dirt dusting polyester fur. But it was cute, different, something to lighten the museum's mood. Everyone who entered the Lost and Found Museum was so somber, reverent, like they were entering a church. All those sacred histories. Or maybe it was just the barn ceilings, echoing and dry, gasping for want of chiming bells.

It was better than what Rod got stuck with for being late too many times: sorting the single gloves and mittens, hanging the scarves and hats. I had to do that when I first started working here. We used to organize those, too, pairing the men's with men's and women's with women's. Rhonda almost did away with the whole display since it was boring to look at and there wasn't much interest in winter accessories this far south. No one knew how half of it ended up here anyway. But every time she got close to tossing it all out, someone would come in and tearfully find a match: the other half to something black and lacy with pearl studs at the wrist, or soft and pastel, hand-knit by a grandmother. Then something like responsibility or guilt would keep it all here.

There are some shoes, too, and every day someone (usually a man in a golf shirt on the far side of middle-aged) comes in and says to us, "How do you suppose anyone loses just one shoe?" and then laughs as if no one has ever said that before. We smile politely and laugh with a slight glint of teeth. Nod. Raise our arms in an exaggerated shrug and say something coy, like *must have been an interesting evening.*

We get idiot questions a lot now in the new location, now that we get people from as far away as Texas. Sometimes we get these hip, pretty people from the city, the kind who wear full makeup with purposefully torn t-shirts and jeans and who keep their cowboy boots pristine. (Rod said to one of these girls: "Y'all know they aren't supposed to look like that, right?") They came wanting to buy things they could resell, especially some of the rarer items: nicer coats trimmed with fur, lace stockings, sunglasses, and handbags and backpacks that looked eclectic or rustic, descriptors that didn't make much actual sense in context. But we didn't sell anything and there was no convincing us to. That wasn't the point, we told them. Rod would then change the subject by way of flirtation. "These are from the late 1960s," he would say, maybe not wrong but definitely bullshitting. "Look through them. Can't you feel it? Can't you feel who used to wear these?"

The newest display, Rhonda's attempt at humor, has every random key we've ever received in a clawfoot bathtub. She put up a sign that says that if you can find one key that opens the lock of the store room door, you win a hundred dollars and a visit to the Adults Only X-Rated section. Many people—mostly teenage boys—have spent hours trying different keys, but none have found the right one among the lost. Rhonda insists the key exists, but the Adults Only X-Rated section certainly doesn't. The hundred dollar prize probably doesn't either.

Now most people come to look at the rarer items, most of which came from hotels or taxis in bigger cities. A Tiffany lamp left in a hotel in Jackson. A portrait of two cats in Victorian clothing left in a rental car that came from Brooklyn to Louisiana. There were two different prosthetic limbs—a left arm and a right foot—from Vero Beach, Florida, and Galveston, Texas, respectively, both from two different airlines. The common question is whether they were from the same person, another stupid one, considering the foot is roughly a men's size fourteen and the hand smaller than mine, small enough to belong to a child. I stuck it on a stuffed bear once, but Rhonda scolded me, told me to take it off.

There were multiple musical instruments, enough for a ragtag band that would blend country and jazz (owing to the one saxophone). There was an accordion a couple of years ago, weighing at least forty pounds, until a German woman in her sixties with a large carpet bag claimed it as her own and no one questioned her.

When people took things, we were supposed to ask them to prove it had once been theirs: a photograph, a receipt. But usually you could just tell, knew by instinct. The relief of recognition is almost impossible to fake, uncomfortable to observe. Like looking into the sun. I know when someone has found something they lost because I can see the world dissolve around them, can feel myself disappearing into soft focus, blending in with the wall of bears and dolls. So we didn't push too hard for proof.

Rhonda still wanted us to do it with the jewelry case, even though I knew she must have kept some of the good shit for herself. There are hundreds of necklaces and bracelets with broken clasps; chains where a single loose link had caused an entire unraveling, a liquid slip from wrist to floor. Watches upon watches, some still ticking but most frozen in a different time: 4:29, 3:16, a perfect 12:00. There are a lot of engagement rings, but less people come looking for those than you'd think. Some of the found things, you learned, were lost on purpose.

Rod and I have worked here since the opening, when it was just a roadside attraction in what used to be a shed that a farmer sold fruit and vegetables out of. Neither of us knew Rhonda then, or how she came to start it in the first place. The jobs had somehow gotten posted on a crusty, neglected bulletin board in our high school right before we graduated.

My getting-out dream was hazy and vague. I wanted to do something More, but the impossibility of it blurred the lines, rendering it like one of the Impressionist paintings we'd looked at in a history class...

Then after a few months, Rhonda got some kind of grant and moved us down the highway into the barn that had been foreclosed on and somehow wasn't condemned. With all of the lost shit in it, it smelled like a library filled with hay.

We both turned nineteen the year of the relocation, and what began as our high school weekend and summer job became our real job, became the rest of our lives, the thing we couldn't get away from. The visitors didn't seem to go far either—the museum was just liminal Louisiana space on the way to an outlet mall or Florida beach or theme park.

Rod's dreams of getting out of our town were more concrete than mine: they involved music and a cousin who lived in Tennessee. My getting-out dream was hazy and vague. I wanted to do something More, but the impossibility of it blurred the lines, rendering it like one of the Impressionist paintings we'd looked at in a history class: less clear the closer you got. So I stayed, decorating with dolls, until it crystallized.

■ ■ ■

In a lull between Friday's lunchtime visitors and the late afternoon, post-beach visitors, Rod nodded to me, and I followed him outside to share in his cigarette. He was trying to stop and I was trying to start so we'd share one, his long drags punctuated by my short puffs. But as we slid the barn door open, we saw the girl standing toward the back of the parking lot, gazing out at a gravel sea.

I felt Rod bristle next to me; both of our necks and backs pulled to attention like puppets attached to the same string. She was about five or six, pale with dark hair, eating a partially-peeled clementine. It was clementine season and we'd learn that she had a bag full of them in the pink vinyl Barbie backpack she carried. It was too heavy for her, pulling her shoulders back, and she teetered on her feet and stumbled slightly when she looked up at me. I stared back at her, and then at Rod, who flattened the cigarette filter between his lips, furrowing his brow. He walked past the girl to the highway and looked around the parking lot, then east and west, shaking his head, then shrugged at me. There was no one and nothing there except for the scent of afternoon rain.

I asked her what her name was, and she didn't answer. I asked if her mama was inside and she shook her head. Dad?

Head shake. Grandma? Head shake. Then she turned and looked back, facing west.

I followed her gaze before I looked at Rod. He shrugged again, his long, gangly limbs flopping to his side like tree branches saturated with rainwater. "Tell Rhonda?" he said, uncertain that any good could come of that. She probably wasn't coming back for the day. Rhonda would be getting her nails done and would come back tomorrow, telling the three other staff members that she'd had a Meeting With Corporate. They didn't know any better—that there was no Corporate. No one had bought us, and most likely no one would—too close to hurricanes and too far from a city. People driving from Texas or Louisiana to Florida. Half the time they didn't even know what state they were in when they pulled into the rocky parking lot. Half the time it didn't matter.

I asked the girl if she wanted to come inside and let me know if she knew anyone there. "You can put your backpack down," I said. "Would that be okay?" She nodded, not looking at me, grown-out brown bangs draped over her eyelids. I slid the door open and led her inside. There were only maybe eight people left in the store at that point. Through the front window I could see the sun setting behind the bald cypress tree past the highway, hazy gold light filtering in through limp tendrils of leaves. No autumn: just a slightly wilted summer.

The path of light was interrupted by Rod re-entering. "Anyone missing a kid?" he said in my direction, but loudly enough that anyone else could have heard him.

"Shh! We're not trying to get her kidnapped. Jesus, Rod."

"Oh. I didn't think about that."

"Because you're a dude. God."

He shrugged and I looked down at the girl. "Can I take your bag?" I asked.

She ignored me, but began to pull her right arm out of its glittery pink strap. I took it from her as it began to sag from her other shoulder, making her teeter to the left. She still had a clementine in her hand and began to pick at its remaining skin with her index finger, gently, like it was a scab that might reopen and spill blood. No one else in the museum seemed to take notice of her. I watched their eyes for sparks of recognition—or deliberate avoidance—but found only momentary distractions from the items lining the walls and shelves. Tiny flecks of orange skin floated to the cement slab of the floor.

I carried the girl's Barbie backpack to the front desk—a corner sectioned off by shelves and a folding table—while Rod wandered back out to the yard. He wasn't one to entertain conflict, even the kind he was paid for. I unzipped the backpack and dug through dozens of clementines looking for an inscribed name. I thought of my mother using a black Sharpie to mark my name in every bag, every jacket, every shoe, every notebook. If I closed my eyes and shut out the smell of the hay and petrichor I could smell her perfume, honeysuckle and jasmine. And the harsh but pleasant chemical smell of the marker. The smell of the need for lost things to find their way home again, some kind of biological instinct, like unique animal cries or nest trimmings.

But there was no name, no initial inscribed on the neon pink, no writing of any kind. Just clementines, some with tiny crescent indentations in them, like the girl had tried several times to find one ripe enough to peel.

I set the bag down next to the clementine girl and opened Rhonda's laptop, directing her browser to a video channel that played cartoons. "This okay?" I said. And she nodded, slowly, wriggling in the chair, one hand pulling her ponytail and one stretching to the side. "Our WiFi is bad," I added. "Sorry."

I wondered if she even spoke English. WiFi seemed universal. I left her and went out the back to find Rod, smoking his cigarette.

"Find her adult supervision yet?" he exhaled fire on to me.

"No. Can you go down to the deli and get her something to eat? A sandwich or something with substance."

"Why do I have to?"

"Because someone has to watch her."

"Why don't you take her with you?"

"Are you serious? So I can get arrested for kidnapping if her parents have been down the road the whole time?"

"Down the road—down the road? Really? Really? Emptiness for miles and you think we'd have missed people looking for a lost child down the road?"

"Maybe. Could be a trap."

"You're fucking paranoid, Leah."

"Anything's possible. Can you just go? The deli or any of the fast food places by the next exit?"

"Waiting for Tad. Getting some—you know. But I can watch her."

"When you aren't exchanging weed at your place of employment? Great."

And that's how I ended up driving myself down I-10, only half looking at other cars that passed me. Driving against the early evening sun, barely able to see. Steering wheel, a few inches of the hood, then blue-white. I kept smelling honeysuckle and jasmine, and hearing some song about a buttermilk sky. I remembered a melody but no word other than those: *buttermilk sky*. If anyone mentioned buttermilk as an ingredient, like buttermilk pancakes, I imagined that liquid-powder blue of early afternoon, a sky softened with light uninterrupted by clouds, and I remembered thinking that pancakes should be blue. Buttermilk blue.

It took twenty minutes to get to the deli by the gas station. I got a packaged peanut butter and jelly sandwich and then I spiraled down a narrow hole of *what if she's allergic to peanuts?* I got cheese as well, even though I knew it would be hot, coated in a film of sweat by the time I got back to the museum.

■ ■ ■

I pulled in to see the short, hourglass shape of Rhonda in the frame of the barn door, one hand resting on the sliding half, but not laying weight on it. I knew because it would screech continuously with the slightest pressure. Rhonda was posing, exercising calm with one half of her body while the other side vibrated with tension: fingernails drumming against the side of her thigh, an ankle flexing and pointing. She had a new wig on, dark barrels of stiff curls. Rod was facing her, his arms gesticulating webs around him, his voice higher than usual. I cut past Rhonda with the sandwiches in a paper bag as he exclaimed, *No, there was no one.* The girl was where I left her at the chair in front of the laptop. Rhonda cut her eyes to me, demanding testimony. I held up the bag with sandwiches.

"She just turned up in the parking lot. We didn't see anyone. She won't say anything to us," I said.

"All right, all right. You both go home," Rhonda sighed. "I'll call the authorities. They'll deal with it."

"Won't they want to talk to us?" I asked.

"Maybe tomorrow. No point in waiting. They take hours to get out here. It's all right," she said, and then, in a stroke of tenderness I'd never quite seen in Rhonda, she went to the girl and squatted down beside the chair and asked: "Do you know what you want to be for Halloween?"

The girl shook her head shyly and Rhonda took her by the hand, leading her over to the lost dolls. The sandwiches grew soggy at the front desk.

■ ■ ■

I opened the next morning at ten, even though no one ever came in until noon or so. I opened the register and Rhonda's laptop, looking at the news to see if anything about a missing girl had been reported. Nothing. I considered safety protocol: how did you advertise a lost child without endangering it? Where did they take them? Who would keep them? I remembered stories about a string of kidnappings across the Gulf South, mostly from these small towns off of highways, populations dwindling with each year as factories closed and more people moved away for jobs and fewer people came back. Others just found the needle or the powder and took themselves off the map, another layer of the coastline washed away. All that was left was the crawfish and the quirky novelties, like us.

I was still scrolling when Rhonda came in, holding Clementine Girl's hand. She looked down at her, then to me, and sighed, exasperated, shiny purple lips squaring with her jaw.

"No reports matching her description in the entire Southeast. She's not in the system. And they can't get anyone from the state child protection here for another couple days since it's the weekend. So, she'll be here. Then sleeping at my house."

"Seriously? They can't take her anywhere?"

"No one cares about this part of the country. Maybe you're too young to remember how clear they made that."

We didn't know much about Rhonda, but we knew that when she talked about the storm that hit thirteen years ago, you didn't push back.

"So what are you gonna do?" I asked.

"Bring her here with me every day, I guess. Can't get no babysitter out here. Maybe someone will recognize her."

"But there are no reports of a missing kid?"

Rhonda shrugged, then led the girl behind the front desk, sitting her in a chair and handing her a Pop-Tart package. "Don't worry about it. Don't you have cleaning to do?"

When I saw Rod's car, I jumped outside and I intercepted him for a cigarette. "Kid's still here," I said, exhaling, the smoke hovering, getting caught in the humidity like a net instead of dissipating. I repeated what Rhonda said and he shook his head.

"Doesn't that seem weird to you? No one from CPS? For a white girl?" he asked.

Others just found the needle or the powder and took themselves off the map, another layer of the coastline washed away. All that was left was the crawfish and the quirky novelties, like us.

"I mean, yeah," I said. Rod had been in the system for longer than I had. If you could call it that.

"I'm just saying—they'd put her on a bus to Texas or South Carolina or something if they didn't have room for her anywhere here."

"But what if they don't have the staff? I don't fucking know," I said. I'd been hogging the cigarette and he snatched it back from me.

"It's Rhonda, man. I don't know."

"What the hell else is she gonna do? It's not like she's keeping her. She isn't a stray kitten."

"Dunno," he said, those long arms flinging the cigarette to the gravel before bouncing back like overused rubber bands. "I'd just think twice."

■ ■ ■

Sunday was the same: the girl sitting and watching videos and eating snacks in a new dress Rhonda found for her at a thrift store and a blue cardigan from our own display. On Mondays we were closed. Tuesday came, and we didn't see Rhonda or the girl. "Maybe she's brought her somewhere," I said to Rod.

"Maybe. Does Rhonda ever come in Mondays?" he asked.

"I think so. Sometimes. To reconcile the week. Financials."

"Can you get into her login?"

"Rod—come on."

"Real quick. I'm not gonna do anything. I just want to check something. Not museum related."

"You're going to get us both fired."

"She isn't coming in. She's never in on Tuesdays. We have fifteen minutes before we open. Just come on."

"Fine," I sighed. I sat down at the laptop and logged in under Rhonda's profile. "What do you want? That's the accounting stuff—that's the ticket information—"

"Nah. Move."

Rod practically sat in my lap before I could move. He opened the browser and went to her email inbox, still logged in from the week before.

"Rod, come on, she's going to know you were poking around in there. She's probably got some kind camera."

He didn't respond, and started scrolling through her inbox. Hundreds of messages, most of them shopping related. Garbage.

"Come on," I said, looking out the front door, my ear trained toward the parking lot. "What are you even looking for?"

"This," he said, and clicked. "Something like this."

■ ■ ■

We didn't wait for a truck with the cameras and a reporter with blown out air to show up before we called the police. We described Rhonda, described the girl. It was true, they had no reports of a missing girl. But they also had no report of a found girl. No call from Rhonda. They had never been contacted at all. Thought Rod and I were crazy or pulling something.

We didn't tell them about Rhonda's emails to the reporters or TV shows she contacted, or how long the girl had actually been there—Rhonda would insist that the girl had only arrived the day before, not the week before. I don't know what was supposed to happen. I don't know why we felt any need to protect Rhonda from trouble, if she was technically in any, if it mattered at all. But by Wednesday morning, an officer and a social worker were at the museum, an hour before opening, waiting for Rhonda and the girl to arrive.

We saw her SUV slow on the highway, then start to pull off in the turning lane. Then we saw her brake abruptly and push her sunglasses to the top of her head. We saw her pull in slowly to the parking lot, hesitant, delaying an inevitable stop. No one wants stories to end, but that is what they do in unmapped towns between the river and the Gulf. End, and end, and end.

Rod and I looked at each other as the cop and social worker began to approach her car. She parked, slid out, plastered a smile on and initiated pleasantries. We watched her unbuckle the girl, hug her closely, and animatedly talk to the cop, not letting him get a word in. I didn't know what she was saying, but while she talked, the social worker put her hand on the girl's back and led her away. The cop led Rhonda to his car, his face hidden by his cap as he wrote something on a pad. As he slid into his car and picked up his radio, Rhonda looked up at us, caught us staring, and furiously pointed toward the barn.

"Guess we're still open," Rod said.

"Yeah, idiot," I responded, though I was equally uncertain about how to proceed.

Walking past Rhonda to get to the door felt like approaching a stray dog. But we trudged through the gravel, Rod sneaking in before me. I paused.

"I'm sorry, Rhonda," I said, quietly and slowly, like I was trying not to blow out a candle.

She glared at me for a moment, and underneath her spidery false eyelashes, I saw the map of all that wandering, all that searching. The job posting for *An Exciting Opportunity* at my and Rod's school. The students more likely to will the town into a new and better place by way of pipes and needles than to actually leave. Rhonda's shimmering nails pressing the tack through that simple white printout on the bulletin board. Those kids made to feel middle-aged at sixteen, to have babies at seventeen, to disappear by twenty. Those numbers made for tearing.

Rhonda slammed her fist against the side of the barn and she hissed, "Oh, yeah, Leah? What do you think? How do you think you got here?" ■

POPPY

The flower clamped
unspeaking before lunch,

its weird alligator-jaw-furled
blazing-pink gullet
wadded up with tissue paper,

    then opening

I wish I'd stayed
to watch you

time-lapse photography revealing
a channel Thirteen thing
crashing into air
a monstrous bloom
teetering on a swizzle stem
a sudden sunlight overdose
of *Little Shop of Horrors* proportions

but I was in the other room when
the poppy opened
just like, in reverse, your heart
clicked closed in the night
without sound, without smell

CAROLYN WILSEY

MARILYN DIPTYCH

After Andy Warhol, Marilyn Diptych, *1962*

a face moving backwards
into history
yellow hair, pink skin
grwying whitefade gone

her curls categorized
in fifty slick technicolor morgues

her mouth a plush red
precision fading to blur

and aqua-sashed eyelids
echoed by arched brows

I think of offstage flesh
the bra gripping her sternum

features stamped on
gelatin halos labeled feminine

I think of the miniaturized Marilyn
alive inside me:
a microchip navigating
my hand toward lipstick

makeup color-blocking
that red aperture mouth

the way it was
all her, never her

CAROLYN WILSEY

FOUR PAINTINGS BY CASSATT

I.

The Pensive Reader, 1894

She doubts it all: the hackneyed lovelorn plot,
soliloquies the brooding stable lad
pontificates to straw, the tedium
of a judge's teenage daughter scheming
her lamp wick down. Our reader sighs, or so
I make her sigh. Her swooping ponytail
fades to auburn brushwork, nebulous
as the hair a jilted suicide unties
to leap so it can splay in mud beside the creek.

II.

Woman Standing, Holding a Fan, 1879

Her dress is muted green with russet flecks
like vines of trellised beans in late July.
Alone, we find the figure's outstretched arm
indulging in a twirl so quick and plain
it does not catch the nearing light that falls
across the chair smothering in lilac blooms.
Victorian, absurdly large, her fan's
perfect scallop arcs, leading to a face
for which a boy would kneel to dare a keyhole peek.

III.

Summertime, 1894

These rowboat drifters lazing on a pond
are sweatless in their heavy sleeves and gloves.

Their season is a floating dream absorbed
in mallards, two, whose rainbow waters lap
impasto orange on pink and violet swirls,
reflectionless. They cannot see their own
faces spectral, wavering in current,
these sisters who have rowed themselves until
the sun-stained sailors clanging by the pier are flecks.

IV.
The Child's Bath, 1893

Our common holiness was always this—
a toddler raven-haired who dips her feet
into a basin where the mischief dirt
from a summer dusk in meadows rambling
will bloom the water dark. Its steam is felt
not seen. The room is middle class mélange,
a floral clash, American. Here is our shrine
to reconcile an ancient faith restyled:
a common mother cradling her common child.

ADAM TAVEL

ELEGY FOR E. A. ROBINSON

Six months and still your parents couldn't name
the boy they wished a girl. They let a crowd
of tipsy cooers at their resort pluck
Edwin from a hat. Of course you earned your Bs
at Harvard, left with no degree, and failed
to woo your brother's fiancée—most lives
can spot themselves in butcher apron stains.
Half of what you penned sad Robinson
just plods, and half of that runs too long. And yet
on nights when gloom, no maudlin thing, knifes through
these rooms like news a fevered child has died
I rouse your spine to ask what might be done.
Down rows of tombs in Tilbury Town you hum
at empty plots, a spade in either palm.

ADAM TAVEL

THIS AMERICAN FIFE

JAKE MAYNARD

The piano may do for love-sick girls who lace themselves to skeletons, and lunch on chalk, pickles and slate pencils. But give me the banjo.

—*Mark Twain*

In 2007, bluegrass banjoist Eddie Adcock did an ordinary thing at an extraordinary time. Robbed of his ability to make music due to involuntary hand tremors, Adcock opted for a risky procedure in which surgeons would install a tiny electrode into the malfunctioning part of his brain. The catch was that to find the exact spot to stick it, Adcock would have to play his banjo while the doctors operated. Or, maybe, the doctors would play the banjo vis-a-vis Adcock's brain. I guess it depends on your perspective.

In the video of the procedure, Adcock, sixties and white, sits with a plastic curtain around his head. A banjo, emblazoned with an American flag on its own head, is practically useless in his hands. Behind the curtain, the surgeons drill and poke and zap the back of his head. All at once, Adcock goes from fumbling to dexterous, mountain twang rolling from his fingers. They move the electrode and the music stops. They move it again. The music returns.

The story made global news; Barbara Walters even covered it. It's easy to see why—an old white man, his loving wife, the feel-good convergence of culture and medicine. And then there's that banjo, that flag. It's hard to image the story being as quaint if he'd played a guitar.

Part of the charm, I think, is that the banjo doesn't seem like the kind of instrument you'd risk your life over. Nat Winston, a psychiatrist and musician from Nashville, wrote that the banjo was "an extrovert of musical instruments, nothing to be thought about, and certainly nothing to be loved except with the *rough-em-up* form of affection you might bestow on a friendly pup." Steve Martin said, "The banjo is such a happy instrument—you can't play a sad song on the banjo—it always comes out so cheerful." The most popular brand of banjo in America is appropriately named *The Goodtime*.

Maybe it's the banjo's appearance. Even the shape is comic: a drum on a stick. On a banjo, the drum is called the pot. The head of the pot is made of skin, stretched so tight that the banjo sings. Because the skin stretches with time and climate, a banjo is always subtly changing its tone. Some ancient banjo pots were made from gourds. Today's are typically made of wood or metal. Occasionally, banjo pots are made from life's trash: salad bowls, hatboxes, the torque converters from 1950s Buicks. Regardless, the skin is what makes a banjo a banjo.

Banjos weren't mass-produced until after the American Civil War, but they quickly became America's most popular instrument. Compared to violins and guitars, they were cheaper and easier to make and repair. Because of the simplicity, a banjo can be disassembled into its constituent parts.

Despite the simplicity, banjos are expressive in design. Some banjo builders inlay silver or goal purfling into the fingerboards. Others are inlaid with detailed abalone images of flowerpots, or sparrows, or creatures from the medieval bestiary. I once played a banjo with a dragon carved along the back of its neck. Another one I played was inlaid with pearlescent spaceships and satellites: the past and future in your hands.

I once played a banjo carved mostly with a pocketknife so that it looked like it was made by a person who only owned a pocketknife. The banjo's owner was a forty-year-old man that I played music with for a few years. He lived with his wife in a tiny house on a long dirt road, past a Confederate cemetery in southern West Virginia. I would drive there in the summer to play fiddle tunes and drink beer on his porch. This was in 2014. They had an outhouse, thirty chickens, and a bellicose peacock. I'd just moved to West Virginia and I used a lot of thesaurus words, like pearlescent and bellicose.

Back then I was playing a Goodtime. Like most banjos, it had a fretted neck like a guitar, allowing the player to finger the same notes consistently. But some banjos—like my friend's—have a smooth, unfretted neck like a violin. The earliest folk recordings feature fretless banjos.

Play a banjo without frets, and the notes slip and slur into one another. Fretless banjos aren't constrained to the twelve-note system of Western musical thought. They contain microtones, the notes where the commas are. Some listeners have internalized the twelve-note system so deeply that they think microtones are just sour notes.

I didn't believe in microtones at first because they weren't discussed in the music books I'd read. But then I was told that I was constrained by the twelve-note system of Western musical thought. So I found a 1920s laminate banjo pot with an unfretted neck. I strung the banjo with nylon strings meant to simulate old-time gut strings. I wanted it to sound archaic; to re-create what one musician called "that old West Virginia graveyard music."

But it wasn't the true past that people like me connected with. It was the heritage...But heritage is also stripped of its contexts and missteps, history's highlight reel.

Unlike the brassy, rollicking bluegrass music most people are familiar with, the songs my friend played were sad or ambivalent, using microtones to alternate between major and minor keys many times in the same song. He said the songs were sad because life in the mountains had been isolating. Midwestern folk music, he said, was happier and more upbeat because life there was more social. I fell in love with old-time banjo music for a while. The heavy syncopation, the ragged edges. The common joke is that old-time music is "so good, it sounds bad."

Rural West Virginia was, in a lot of ways, like the tiny town I was from in Upper Pennsylvania—clannish, run-down, and charming. But unlike my part of Pennsylvania, in West Virginia the folk music traditions had been preserved. But it wasn't the true past that people like me connected with. It was the heritage. You know, the part of history that assumes the past won't be remembered on its own, so it makes something so remarkable that we have to keep it. But heritage is also stripped of its contexts and missteps, history's highlight reel. While I didn't see it at the time, I loved that old Appalachian mountain sound because everyone said it was white and rural and lost, which was how I saw myself.

■ ■ ■

There are many ways to play a banjo. Ragtime and blues players liked to thwap their banjos with plectrums, choking the strings to limit reverberation. Irish musicians like to note fast, articulate melodies in unison with a fiddle or fife. Bluegrass players roll their fingers over the strings in syncopated patterns of three and four, tickling the strings.

Most tradition Appalachian musicians play with a highly specific style called clawhammer, in which the index finger flicks single notes while the thumb and remaining fingers play drones and shifting chords. With clawhammer style you can play the rhythm and melody. You are you own accompaniment—perfect for an isolated place.

To understand clawhammer's rhythm, read this out loud:

Claw hammer. Claw hammer.
Or:
1 ( ) 3 4 5 ( ) 7 8.
Or:
Bum ditty. Bum ditty.

I started playing clawhammer banjo in college. There'd been some seniors on campus my freshman year. They played old-time country music and were radical environmentalists—almost as hillbilly as hippie. It was my first time seeing those two things together. Most of my old hometown friends had become loggers, and these kids were more likely to chain themselves to construction equipment. Some of them, it turned out, were rich kids. But that was okay. They represented a convergence of the things I'd been and things I wanted to be. And the banjo symbolized it perfectly.

I bought my Goodtime and learned the clawhammer style from a Smithsonian documentary featuring clips of Black migrant farmers and poor white southerners playing their songs for an ethnographer's lens. I remember that documentary clearly. I watched it in my sterile cinderblock dorm room in the spring of 2007, wearing my father's flannel shirt. My hair was long and I'd just stuck a sticker on my banjo case actually, literally said "This Machine Kills Fascists." On the screen men sang about their troubles: crop damage, heartache, addiction, poverty, loss. My family had real troubles, too. Lives as similar to the singers as they were to mine. My father had sold timber from our property to buy my textbooks; our hometown was puckering like an old apple; my sister's husband was a mean drunk. But I didn't think of those things back then. I was too busy toting around the banjo, sitting in the grass of the campus quad, sandals strewn beside me, practicing those first few songs while people walked by and asked: *is that a banjo?*

Yeah, I told them. This was cultural preservation, an act of defiance against modern commodification of music. I was getting in touch with my roots.

And in a way, I was. The word banjo may be portmanteau of banza (an African instrument) and the Caribbean verb banja—meaning to play the fool.

■ ■ ■

There are few images as closely tied with white rural life as the banjo. Think *Deliverance*. Think *Beverly Hillbillies*. Think *Little House on the Prairie*. But the banjo's origins are syncretic. The banjo, or its predecessors, arrived in North America via the West African slave trade. Early American records brim with accounts of slaves playing the banjo. An enslaved person's musical skills were often mentioned when they were bought and sold. In the Caribbean, enslaved people were disallowed from playing drums (drums could be used to signal revolts) so slaves stuck to banjos and flutes, sometimes adopting European fifes.

The banjo was associated with Black people for most of what we call American History. It's only for the last 120 years or so that the banjo has been thought of as a white, rural instrument. But even when whites weren't playing the thing, we were its arbiters. One eighteenth-century musician, a freed Black man named Banjo Billy, was remembered by an admirer in the *New York Times* as "a famous banjo player. And not the fanciful instruments of today, handled by cork-faced counterfeits, but the genuine banjo of the Negro." Then, like now, the gates to authenticity were closely guarded.

White people probably first started playing the banjo on plantations, but "the cork-faced counterfeits" of minstrel shows were likely the first white people to perform with a banjo. Covered in blackface (often made from charred cork) white minstrels sang songs like "Darkie's Delight," "The Free N——r," and "Genuine Negro Jig." One of the primary themes of minstrel shows—like today's country music—was nostalgia. Minstrels were targeting white audiences who wanted to remember slavery as a happy and carefree existence for Black Americans. Even in its heyday, the banjo was concerned with the past.

The supposed progenitor of the minstrel show, a military fife player from Ohio named Dan Emmett, put together his first band, "The Virginia Minstrels" in New York City in the 1840s. Best known for writing "Dixie," which became a rallying cry for the Confederacy, Emmett learned much of his repertoire from a white West Virginia man named Archibald Ferguson. (At the time, West Virginia was still a part of Virginia.) Emmett hired Ferguson to work with his traveling show and, as soon as he'd learned all of Ferguson's techniques and tunes, Emmett fired him, writing that Ferguson was "very ignorant and n——r all over, except in color."

The mimesis gets even more fucked up from there. After emancipation, it was common for African-American musicians to enter minstrelsy because it paid much better than performing for Black audiences. These performers typically wore blackface and white gloves so they would pass as white men trying to look like Black men, not Black men trying to look like white men trying to look like Black men. Men also performed as women. One of the first female impersonators, George Christy, was famous for his performance of a mixed-race seductress named Lucy Long. While cavorting around the stage, he'd narrate Lucy's pursuit of men from multiple points of view, singing, "If she becomes a scolding wife / as surely she was born / I'll take her down to Georgia / and trade her off for corn."

■ ■ ■

In the old-time music community, it's common to hear that "the banjo came from Africa," which is a subtle whitewash, winking at the past without ever having to look hard at it. It's more accurate to say that the banjo's history is a long tangle of appropriation, re-appropriation, exchange, and

theft, reimagined by the cultures it passed through. Like many traditions of the poor, the banjo became faddish at times.
In the Victorian era, the banjo became the rage among the wealthy urbanites, and rich kids took banjo lessons in their fine mahogany parlors. Later, leftist folkies like Pete Seeger sought to turn the instrument against its history. On the head of his banjo, he optimistically wrote, "This machine surrounds hate and forces it to surrender."

Suffice it to say, the banjo is quintessentially American—messy, fraught, and baffling. "Nobody owns an instrument," argues Rhiannon Giddens, a founding member of all-Black string band The Carolina Chocolate Drops, who upended the folk music scene with their interpretations of early Black country music. Giddens has become a significant voice in public discourse about tradition, receiving a MacArthur Fellowship in 2017. Decidedly broad, her work spans original songs, slave ballads, Appalachian mountain music, early blues and jazz, and occasionally Gaelic music. "No culture gets to put the lockdown on anything," she says.

This idea encapsulates the state of the banjo in the postmodern era. Shunned from country for sounding too country, it's found a home with the indie songsters, old-time revivalists, and experimental musicians. Today's banjoists play bluegrass alongside Beethoven, slave songs alongside Taylor Swift. Bela Fleck, who has been credited with innovative banjo work in jazz and classical music, produced a 2008 documentary called *Throw Down Your Heart*, in which he travels to Africa and collaborates with traditional musicians, working to bridge American bluegrass with African banjo traditions. It's a positive, if privileged, quest to understand the instrument's history.

It's hard not to catch a whiff of appropriation when you hear pop darlings like Mumford and Sons strumming their banjos. But authenticity is more of a feeling than it is an objective reality, and who am I to say, anyway? I still don't know what to do with the instrument and its history. My old Goodtime sits unplayed in a closet. I'm not sure if I'll play again. But, if I do, the best thing I can do is play with more awareness and grace than before. "They think the banjo can only be happy," Fleck says in *Throw Down Your Heart*. "But that's not true." ■

The research for this essay comes mostly from two books: *The Banjo: America's African Instrument* by Laurent Dubois and *I Hear America Singing: Folk Music and National Identity* by Rachel Clare Donaldson. Additional research comes from *The Quest for Authenticity in Popular Music* by Hugh Barker and Yaval Taylor; *Earl Scruggs and the Five-String Banjo* by Earl Scruggs; "Rhiannon Giddens and What Folks Music Means" by John Jeremiah Sullivan; the *New York Times* digital archives; and through time spent at folk music festivals.

I SWAM INTO YOU BY ACCIDENT

The Blue Line trail is all cool indirection:
it skirts beaten paths and levees,
leads through bogs that sink footprints
and erases the traces of passage
begrudging return, as who
wouldn't want to stay where broken bottles
settle scores on the rocky shore
of a lake supposed to be haunted.
A busted pump house juts from an outcrop.
Faded graffiti hints at petroglyphs
of spiral jetties in a smooth
windward wall. Looking vaguely
pre-Navajo. In one breath a starry encounter
a nest of threads at antennae-like
angles and the careless
could be in for a swim. Maybe find
an underwater cave and come out in Ohio.
Maybe get tangled up in
mangrove roots. Or stay on the path,
vary the length of a measure, leap
through hollows and spin a new cocoon.

GERALD YELLE

YOU GO HERE

You take the slope at an inadvisable angle
tipping the tractor and pinning your leg.
It hurts and worse: you get
to mull the foolishness that got you here.
Wildflowers line the ruts between rows
of freshly planted corn. Some things you only
see with your face to the ground like this.
You crashed your bike through the cellar door
where you worked two summers ago
walking off without a scratch.
They called you Evel Knievel which almost
made up for having to work for free
to pay for the damage you did
—it went straight to your head though
and led straight here, where when the tractor
began to tip you kicked your leg out
as if to hold up a bike, and now
you wonder if you'll bleed out or pass out
or if the leg will be lost or useless.
No one hears your call for help from this
field on your girlfriend's father's farm
in the middle of nowhere, a world away
from the place you were so glad
to escape. The house is half a mile off
and after a while your voice gives out.
You hum songs in your head while you wriggle
and dig the rocks and dirt out from
under your leg and it rains and the minutes
become hours and you dig and wiggle until you
can pull yourself free. A little more than
a month and you walk without a crutch.

Only a small bruise to your ego
where your girl married a friend with your
same first name, which might save her
some occasional embarrassment or
confusion in bed. The leg aches in damp
and they call you Chester and they call you
Hop-Along and they find it hard to
fathom how you still manage to swagger.

GERALD YELLE

OLD WOMAN
AT MY WINDOW

ELAINE NEIL ORR

It's six a.m. on an April morning. I sit at my desk before the window, ready to write. The first thing I see are dogwood flowers. They appear suspended like lanterns over water. Eventually, tree branches come into view. I look down at my writing and when I look back up, the window is greening. The color emerges by the moment. More green, more shades of green, greater intensities of green, as if my window is a kaleidoscope of greens, even on this cloudy morning.

■ ■ ■

I lift my coffee cup and feel a kink in my wrist. I am becoming old. My skin sags in all kinds of places. My hair thins; lips too; even my fingernails. Brown splotches that were endearing on my parents now show up on my face overnight. When I hit my arm against the porcelain sink, I bleed. So now I truly am thin-skinned. I start looking for swimsuits with sleeves so my sagging arms won't show. I've settled into a permanent weight, not overweight. But I'm not svelte and if I were, more places would sag.

■ ■ ■

A robin lights on the crepe myrtle outside my window. Its early leaves are the size of squirrels' ears and brown-green, almost autumnal. The slender branches stand out like a minimalist water color whereas the sugar maple is thick thick thick with spring green leaves. It rained last night. The morning sky is still gray. Wind sets the limbs of the dogwood dancing, and the oak and the sugar maple. Have you seen the way limbs dip in the wind, move out, dip again and arch, like dancers?

■ ■ ■

When I get up from my desk after sitting too long, I take a few steps like a cowpoke before I can stand up straight. I'm glad no one is watching but the dog. Is this why April is cruel? My eyelids dip. They do not then leap and arch. I need a second cup of coffee.

■ ■ ■

The dogwood is aging. Moss grows along its limbs. The flowers are not as large as they used to be when they filled the entire living room window like a cloud so that looking out one thought one was in an airplane—or an aeroplane, if we want to be dreamy. Every year more dead wood appears and we trim it back. But the main branches still stretch out and up and every year, a few new shoots appear.

The sun is trying to push its way through the clouds. The green on the crepe myrtle springs to gold. A shaft of light hits the neighbor's lawn.

Now a tufted titmouse appears on a branch five feet from my window, holding a golden leaf in its beak. For a nest, no doubt, the leaf brittle from wintering. But the sun slides back behind the clouds, or, more accurately, the clouds close over it. Still, the view from my window has yellowed. A bird streaks by so fast I can't tell its species. I think of my granddaughter. She streaks by, running like a colt. The sun tries again; the world lightens; again the clouds close over it.

■ ■ ■

I'm only sixty-six. My mother retired when she was sixty-one. How spry she seemed, walking with me when I was twenty-eight. She wore knee-length shorts and bright tops; her hair salt and pepper. Of course she looked old to me but I was still in the bloom of youth and having excellent sex. We walked stride in stride.

■ ■ ■

The sun is out in full. I have to close the shades in the upper part of the window. Another bird streaks by. Because it rained last night, the leaves now shimmer with water drops. All those years I sat in the sun, sun-bathing. I never believed the warnings because who would when her legs are long and lithe and her long thick hair falls past her shoulders and every walk across campus is full of her own erotic aura. She is so full of herself.

■ ■ ■

I give myself flowers. Every week. To adorn this desk in front of the window, to adorn me. An ad slips into my email telling me I can have five-star panties, five for thirty-nine dollars. Blue sky appears in the wedge of sky between the trees. The birds swoop quickly. So many of them. There's the cardinal, my most reliable visitor through the winter. In his last year, my father had trouble lifting his right foot to walk. The red bird lingers, looks at me, his beak orange as an orange. The neighborhood street is silver now.

■ ■ ■

Spring means sloughing off the layers of winter: silk underwear, long-sleeved sweaters, long pants, coats. On a day last week when the temperature reached eighty, I put on shorts and a T-shirt. My skin is so white. Who knew that the skin and muscle on forearms could sag? It frightens me to think what people see when I'm not posing. I envy the birds their feathers. Now there's a towhee in the crepe myrtle, that mischief maker who hops up and lands with both feet, scratching backwards to find its favorite foods, sending dead leaves and pine straw all over my sidewalk.

■ ■ ■

I am not as clever as Virginia Woolf. I haven't written about the dying moth and intimations of mortality but the whole blooming world.

But now watch. I will take the dog for a walk. The wind will fill my hair and the owl will sing its morning hoo-hoo. Daily, the dog and I walk two miles in the neighborhood. I'll reflect on my writing about the woman at my window who writes with weathered hands. Later in the day, I'll squat with my granddaughter at the garden creek. We'll take our shoes off and stand in the cold spring water and wiggle our toes. In her laughter she will clutch me. We won't fall. ■

BOOK REVIEWS

Valerie Nieman. *To the Bones*. Morgantown, W.Va.: West Virginia University Press, 2019. 220 pages. Softcover. $19.99.

Reviewed by Katherine Scott Crawford

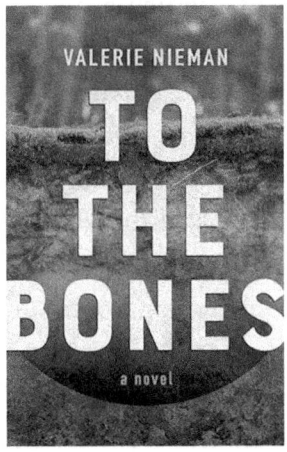

The images in Valerie Nieman's novel *To the Bones*—dank mine shafts rattling with skeletons, acidic rivers peeling the skin from human faces, gaping head wounds, and more—should make us all want to turn back. This was my first thought, upon reading the jacket copy: Are not the horrors coal mining inflicts upon the American landscape enough, without a hint of zombie?

The answer is quick: No. Not nearly enough. Nieman does not take her readers gently into the West Virginia night. She plummets us down mine shafts, walks us through grand and terrifying old houses, sends our cars skidding over lonely mountain roads, hides us in dusty attics, makes us watch characters to whom we've become attached melt before our eyes. Hers is a heart-pounding, cinematic, and multi-layered story. It's the sort of rollercoaster ride you race back to the start of the line for, time and again, because despite a queasy stomach and your heart in your throat, you're not ready for the thrill to end.

From the moment Darrick Brehon, orphan, government auditor and unlikely hero, wakes in a mine shaft filled with dead bodies, to the story's very last line, I was in, too: a community member of hardscrabble Redbird, West Virginia, on the hunt for the truth. How did Darrick end up in that awful crack in the earth? Who were the skeleton dead, recent and otherwise? Did an evil more profligate than acid seep into the water from mining tunnels beneath the town? Why was he now possessed of a dangerous power? And what did the controlling and cryptic Kavanaugh family have to do with any of it?

It is to Nieman's storytelling credit that she then introduces sharp and steady Louranna Taylor, a Redbird native and sweepstakes operator on the search for her missing daughter. Louranna is a fighter, tough as her mountain roots, and a well-drawn equal to Darrick and the novel's other central characters, including conflicted ex-Marine Marco DeLucca and persistent local journalist Zadie Person. Nieman mines the interiority of her characters to glance a flashlight's beam off their flinty layers. Characters who so easily could become stock—whether by trade or regional stereotype—are instead revealed to be deeply human. Put them on a quest—to unlock the secrets behind the poisoning of their town, save their family members, and usurp a dangerous, robber-baron-like ruling family—and give it a supernatural twist, and the novel becomes something entirely new and different.

My favorite books are those which straddle the genre line, refusing to exist within publishing industry parameters. *To the Bones* does exactly this, and while one of its genres is certainly

Appalachian literature, it defies expected themes. Take frustrated outsider Darrick, who halfway through the story asks this internal question of his West Virginia compatriots: "How much misery could one place absorb? Disappearances, murders, mine disasters, people dying in a river that might have boiled right out of hell? Why don't people just leave?"

This is the question, right? Most Appalachian, regional, and place-based literature in general concerns itself on some level with an unapologetic love of the land. But instead of offering us the land and its beauty, Nieman offers us its people. Like Louranna, who tells Darrick that, "... we still love these hills, more'n you can imagine. We make a home here because it is home, not because it's easy. We grow up learning to fish, hunt ramps, shake down apples. We build our homes in places that don't make economic sense. And we dig coal, because that's what we've done for generations, and there's pride in having the skill and guts to do that even when we know the cost." Louranna, however, is the only character who seems to voice why she stays. If the others have their reasons, they never fully emerge from the dark, and perhaps do not really need to.

It is this purposeful rattling back and forth between terror and beauty which makes *To the Bones* a frank surprise of a novel. Not every writer can move with believable success between describing the dead in a ruined river, their eyes "... milky globes in raw, red sockets," to a love scene wherein the woman reveals "the ladder of her ribs" to a man who feels he "... might climb to heaven." But Nieman guides us along these narrative switchbacks with skill and temerity.

Like a miner following a coal seam underground, a deep read of this novel will offer up a variety of thematic paths:

a dive into Irish mythology, a horror of environmental devastation, a study of human internal conflict, even a riff on the paranormal. Nieman pairs sharp, intellectual prose with masterful plotting, and the end result is rip-roaring story—the very definition of a literary page-turner.

I read *To the Bones* into a succession of nights, dreamt of it, and thought about it upon waking. When you pick it up, be ready with a strong stomach, a chunk of free time where everyone leaves you the heck alone, and a long-burning nightlight. ∎

A POET OF HOPE

But what if
that famous writer
had grown up
in my
shit brick
suburbs
built over corn
and alfalfa
when
federal initiatives
consumed poor
ethnic enclaves
and pushed us from urban cores?
Could he be a pastoralist
for garden boxes
would he mourn for
my Nonna
who couldn't raise chickens
would he be halted
by cracks in the pavement
the popping of tar
with red pennies,
would the breaking
of blacktop
by varicose roots
remind him
of broken bread?
Make him a
poet of hope?
I have my doubts,
shit brick suburban

raised over fields
which before that
were forests
and seas.

CHRIS COCCA

CONTRIBUTORS

Chris Cocca's fiction, essays, and poetry have been published in *Hobart, Brevity, Pindeldyboz, elimae, Geez,* and *The Huffington Post.* He is a recipient of the Creager Prize for Creative Writing at Ursinus College and completed his MFA in Creative Writing at The New School.

Katherine Scott Crawford is the author of the historical novel *Keowee Valley.* A newspaper columnist, essayist, college English teacher, and former backpacking guide, her work has appeared in *South Loop Review, Santa Fe Writer's Project: The Journal, Wilderness House Literary Review,* and in newspapers including *USA Today, Detroit Free Press,* and *Herald Scotland.* A fellowship recipient of the North Carolina Arts Council, she holds an MFA from Vermont College of Fine Arts. Crawford is founder and director of MountainTop Writers Retreats, located in the mountains of Western North Carolina, where she lives with her husband and daughters.

Carey Gough is a Lexington, Kentucky-based documentary and fine art photographer. Her images are often contemplations on the point in which documentary photography mingles with poetry, cultural memory, and mythology. Her work has been exhibited in both the United States and the United Kingdom, and has been featured on vice.com, noisey.com, *Oxford American*'s Eyes on the South, and RawFile. She teaches at the University of Kentucky, primarily teaching darkroom techniques.

A native of Buckhannon, West Virginia, **Jimmy Long** earned an English degree from Marietta College in 1993. In recent years he has resumed an active writing life in Charleston, where he works and lives with his family of five. Long's work has appeared in *Appalachian Review, Roanoke Review,* and *Still: The Journal.* His poems will also appear in forthcoming editions of *Kestrel* and *Appalachian Journal.*

Laura Marshall is a New Orleans native and longtime New Yorker currently based in Los Angeles, and she holds an MFA in Creative Writing from Hunter College. Her work appears or is forthcoming in *Salon, Reductress, Kestrel, Raleigh Review, Tiferet,* and *The Chattahoochee Review* as a 2020 Lamar York Prize finalist in nonfiction.

Jake Maynard's writing appears in *The New York Times, Guernica, Slate, Chattahoochee Review,* and many other publications. He's from rural Pennsylvania and won't stop talking about it.

Laura Neal is an African-American poet from South Carolina greatly influenced by social and environmental narratives. She received her BA from Bowie State University and her MFA from the University of Maryland College Park. Her work has been published in Academy of American Poets, *Birmingham Poetry Review,* and *Boston Art Review,* among others. She has received fellowships from the Fine Arts Work Center, CALLALOO, Hambidge Center for Creative Arts, and Juniper Writing Institute. She currently teaches creative writing at the University of Texas in Dallas.

Elaine Neil Orr is professor of English at North Carolina State University in Raleigh, where she teaches world literature and creative writing. She also serves on the faculty of the low-residency MFA in Writing program at Spalding University in Louisville. Author of *A Different Sun,* two scholarly books, and the memoir *Gods of Noonday: A White Girl's African Life,* she has been a featured speaker and writer-in-residence at numerous universities and conferences and is a frequent fellow at the Virginia Center for the Creative Arts. She grew up in Nigeria.

Natasha Pepperl's work has appeared or is forthcoming in *Lily Poetry Review, The Meadow, The Maynard, The Anti-Languorous Project,* and elsewhere. She hosts *Just As Special,* a foster care podcast focused on diversity, and is the daughter of an Iranian refugee. Read more of Natasha's poetry at CeremoniesOfFamily.com.

Erin Miller Reid is a dermatologist living in Kingsport, Tennessee. Her poetry and fiction have been published in *Still: The Journal,* where her short story "The Offering" won the publication's 2018 fiction contest. Her work has also been included in the Women of Appalachia Project's annual anthology, *Women Speak.* She is currently writing her first novel.

Shawna Kay Rodenberg holds an MFA from the Bennington Writing Seminars. Her reviews and essays have appeared in *Consequence, Salon, Village Voice,* and *Elle*. In 2016, Rodenberg was awarded the Jean Ritchie Fellowship, the largest monetary award given to an Appalachian writer, and in 2017 she was the recipient of a Rona Jaffe Foundation Writer's Award. A registered nurse, community college English instructor, mother of five, and grandmother of one, she lives on a hobby goat farm in southern Indiana. Her debut memoir, *Kin,* is forthcoming in June 2021.

Adam Tavel is the author of four books of poetry, including the forthcoming *Sum Ledger* (Measure Press, 2021). His most recent collection, *Catafalque,* won the Richard Wilbur Award (University of Evansville Press, 2018). You can find him online at www.adamtavel. com.

Carolyn Wilsey loves living within walking distance of the continent's edge. Nature, art, relationships, and life's mystical qualities inspire her to write poems. The recipient of an MFA in creative writing, fiction, from Emerson College, her work can be found in *Pretty Owl Poetry, Rogue Agent, Stirring,* and *The Virginia Normal,* and is forthcoming in *West Marin Review.*

Gerald Yelle is a member of the Florence, Massachusetts Poets Society and lives in Amherst, Massachusetts. His books include *The Holyoke Diaries,* and *Mark My Word and the New World Order.* He has an e-chapbook titled *Industries Built on Words* at Yavaneka Press and a chapbook titled *No Place I Would Rather Be* forthcoming from Finishing Line Press.